THE GULF CRISIS:
The View from Qatar

The Gulf Crisis
The View from
Qatar

Edited by
Rory Miller

دار جامعة حمد بن خليفة للنشر
HAMAD BIN KHALIFA UNIVERSITY PRESS

Hamad Bin Khalifa University Press
P O Box 5825
Doha, Qatar

www.hbkupress.com

ISBN: 978-9927129599

Printed in Beirut-Lebanon

Qatar National Library Cataloging-in-Publication (CIP)

The Gulf crisis: the view from Qatar / editor Roy Miller. – Doha: Hamad Bin Khalifa University
Press, 2018.

Pages ; cm

ISBN: 978-9927-129-59-9

1. Qatar politics and government – 21st century. 2. Qatar foreign relations – 21st century. I.
Miller, Roy, editor. II. Title.

DS247.Q38 G84 2018

953.63–dc23   201827085120

Abbreviations

AFP	Agence France-Presse
AP	Associated Press
ASEAN	Association of Southeast Asian Nations
CAABU	Council for Arab-British Understanding
CIRS	Center for International and Regional Studies
DICID	Doha International Center for Interfaith Dialogue
EU	European Union
FAO	Food and Agriculture Organization
FPPMS	Forum for Promoting Peace in Muslim Societies
GCC	Gulf Cooperation Council
GCCIA	GCC Interconnection Authority
GECF	Gas Exporting Countries Forum
GEM	Global Entrepreneurship Monitor
HBKU	Hamad Bin Khalifa University
ILO	International Labour Organization
ISIS	Islamic State of Iraq and the Levant
IUMS	International Union of Muslim Scholars
KISR	Kuwait Institute for Scientific Research
LNG	Liquefied Natural Gas
MEC	Ministry of Economy and Commerce
MENA	Middle East and North Africa
MME	Ministry of Municipality and Environment
MOI	Ministry of Interior

NGO	Non-Governmental Organization
NIAG	National Information Assurance Glossary
OBG	Oxford Business Group
OPEC	Organization of the Petroleum Exporting Countries
PETA	Power Exchange and Trade Agreement
QBIC	Qatar Business Incubation Center
QCRI	Qatar Computing Research Institute
QDB	Qatar Development Bank
QF	Qatar Foundation
QIA	Qatar Investment Authority
QNA	Qatar News Agency
QNB	Qatar National Bank
QNRF	Qatar National Research Fund
QNV	Qatar National Vision 2030
QP	Qatar Petroleum
SME	Small and Medium Enterprise
UAE	United Arab Emirates
VAT	Value-Added Tax
VPN	Virtual Private Network
WEF	World Economic Forum
WISE	World Innovation Summit for Education

Contents

Introduction: *The Gulf Crisis: The View from Qatar*
Rory Miller, Georgetown University in Qatar......................9

Section 1: *Economics, Politics and Society*............................17

Adapting Ambitions at the Time of Crisis: Qatar's International Cultural Strategies
Karen Exell, University College London (UCL) Qatar.................19

Food Security: The Case of Qatar
Tareq Al-Ansari, Hamad Bin Khalifa University..........................28

Entrepreneurship in Qatar: Is the Blockade a Golden Opportunity?
M. Evren Tok, Hamad Bin Khalifa University..............................39

Religious Arguments and Counter-Arguments During the Gulf Crisis.
Sohaira Z. M. Siddiqui, Georgetown University in Qatar...............49

The Domestic Policy Opportunities of an International Blockade
Jocelyn Sage Mitchell, Northwestern University in Qatar 58

Qatar Foundation: A Civil Society Actor Responds to a Crisis
Maryah B. Al-Dafa, Hamad Bin Khalifa University......................69

Section 2: *International Affairs* 87

Qatar, the Gulf Crisis and Small State Behavior in International Affairs
Rory Miller, Georgetown University in Qatar.............................89

The Qatar Crisis through the Lens of Foreign Policy Analysis
Gerd Nonneman, Georgetown University in Qatar.......................98

Cyber Security in Qatar and the Gulf Crisis
Joseph J. Boutros, Texas A&M University at Qatar......................109

The Gulf Crisis and the Gulf Gas Markets: The Qatari Perspective
Steven Wright, Hamad Bin Khalifa University............................119

International Energy Law and the Gulf Crisis
Damilola S. Olawuyi, Hamad Bin Khalifa University 127

The Other Gulf Cold War: GCC Rivalries in Africa
Harry Verhoeven, Georgetown University in Qatar *136*

Section 3: *The Crisis in the Media* *145*

Twitter as an Instrument of Foreign Policy: *Qatar and the GCC*
Banu Akdenizli, Northwestern University in Qatar *147*

The Editorialization of "Hard News" Reports in the Gulf Crisis: *A Case*
Study in the Politics of Translation
Ashraf Fattah, Hamad Bin Khalifa University *157*

How International Media Tackled the Blockade
Christina Paschyn, Northwestern University in Qatar *168*

Index *179*

Introduction:

THE GULF CRISIS: THE VIEW FROM QATAR
RORY MILLER, GEORGETOWN UNIVERSITY IN QATAR

On a Monday morning in early June 2017, without any specific forewarning, Saudi Arabia, the United Arab Emirates (UAE) and Bahrain abruptly cut off diplomatic ties, closed their borders and airspace, and suspended all flights to and from Qatar. This move by three of Qatar's closest economic and security partners was backed up by Egypt and a group of smaller states. In Doha, initial concerns revolved around the availability of fresh food, which before the crisis had been supplied to the country's stores by road from Saudi Arabia. There was also a sudden drop in the value of the stock market and heightened concerns over the ambitious plans for the FIFA football World Cup scheduled to take place in Qatar in 2022 – the first time an Arab or Muslim nation will host the world's biggest sporting event.

The economy and financial sector were subsequently stabilized at considerable expense, new domestic and overseas sources of supply were established, the building of roads, railways and stadia continued, and daily life returned to normal for most. What has taken longer to come to terms with is the realization that some of Qatar's closest neighbors, who share intricate and complex family and business ties, as well as a common language, religion and history, had chosen to break ties the way they did in the summer of 2017.

Throughout the blockade, the Qatari government has adopted a consistent position in response to the claims made against it. It has categorically rejected the accusation that it supports terrorism and has defended relations with Iran, Islamists and others in terms of its independent foreign policy and long-time commitment to dialogue. To counter such claims further, it has also highlighted Qatar's status as home to two of America's most important overseas military bases, which play a key role in the US-led air war against Islamic State in Syria and Iraq. At the same time, the government has repeatedly offered to engage with the blockading countries in order to find a solution acceptable to all parties. "We are willing to sit and talk," explained Foreign Minister Sheikh Mohammed bin Abdulrahman Al Thani in an interview with CNN early in the crisis, though he made clear "that attempts to impose policies are out of the question."

A year on, this remains the position of the Qatari government. One argument in particular has been very effective in influencing international opinion: that Qatar is the victim of a direct assault on its national sovereignty by a coalition of much larger powers, whose actions have undermined security in the Arab Gulf, a region that before the blockade was an oasis of stability in the wider Arab world. In these terms, the crisis has not only had important long-term implications for life in Qatar. It has also cast a giant shadow over future relations between Gulf neighbors under the auspices of the Gulf Cooperation Council (GCC), which has been undermined by events.

Although a far from perfect institution, for four decades until the blockade the GCC had contributed to regional economic and security cooperation and had fostered prosperity, development and mutual understanding. Now the GCC's future is uncertain at a time of grave insecurity and crisis in Yemen, Syria and across the wider region. This is particularly problematic as the blockade has also greatly impacted on the security architecture and alliance system between Washington and its key local allies in one of the world's most important regions.

Domestically, early reactions to the blockade among the country's 2.5 million inhabitants – citizens and foreign residents alike – were of surprise verging on disbelief. There was particular shock that the launch of the blockade was timed to coincide with the first full week of Ramadan, usually a peaceful time in the Muslim world. An even bigger shock since then has been the extreme hostility expressed toward Qatar and its leadership by government officials and the media in blockading countries. This has resulted in a sort of "social trauma" that will take a long time to overcome, but it has also fostered solidarity among citizens and the large expatriate community.

Hamad Bin Khalifa University, a public research university founded in 2010 by Qatar Foundation, Qatar's oldest and most important civil society actor, commissioned this volume in recognition of the significant impact that the blockade has had on the domestic, regional and international levels. I would like to thank HBKU President Dr. Ahmad M. Hasnah and project director Marya Al-Dafa for their support in this endeavor. I would also like to thank Rima Ismail of HBKU Press for overseeing the book's publication. I offer special thanks to Rodolphe Boughaba, who had the original idea for this volume and who has been hugely supportive and helpful in seeing it to fruition over subsequent months.

All the chapter contributors are Doha-based scholars and experts working at the various universities and research institutions hosted in Qatar under the auspices of Qatar Foundation. I would like to thank my colleagues at Georgetown University in Qatar, Northwestern University in Qatar, Texas A&M University at Qatar, University College London (UCL) Qatar, and Hamad Bin Khalifa University for their enthusiastic support for this project and for the range and depth of expertise that they have brought to these pages. They are social and political scientists, engineers and economists, experts on security and diplomacy, scholars of Islam and linguistics, and authorities on culture and the arts. Their combined local knowledge and their cutting-edge research are showcased here in a series of policy-oriented analysis pieces that address a wide range of topics and issues in a reader-friendly style that is easily accessible to a general audience.

The 15 chapters in this volume are divided into three sections. The first section offers insider accounts of the ways the crisis has influenced Qatar's economy, politics and society. The second frames the crisis in its important international context. The third looks at the ways the crisis has been covered in traditional and social media outlets and how the various parties to the conflict and their supporters have used the media to promote their own positions.

Section one begins with a study of the impact of the crisis on Qatar's globally significant cultural and creative industries, which have become an important vehicle for the country's branding, global visibility and relevance over the last decade and a half. Here Karen Exell shows how, at the outset of the crisis, there was international consensus around the view that hostilities would be wholly detrimental to Qatar's cultural and artistic life. Though the blockade has had some challenging resource impacts and has led to the reduction of regional cultural interactions, she shows how Qatar has adapted its cultural strategies to deal with the new environment.

The following two chapters by Tareq Al-Ansari and M. Evren Tok argue that the post-embargo era is a potential turning point, respectively, for food security and entrepreneurial endeavors in Qatar. Al-Ansari notes that the debate on food security inside Qatar long predated the blockade. The importance of ensuring the security and sustainability of food, as well as energy and water, increasingly occupies the thinking of decision-makers in sovereign states across the globe, and is an especially pressing matter in countries such as Qatar that face a scarcity of water and severe climate patterns. That said, as Al-Ansari shows, the blockade has played an important role in fostering further consensus over the urgency of accelerating plans that prioritize increased domestic food production within a sustainable development framework.

M. Evren Tok makes a similar point in his chapter on the impact of the blockade on Qatar's entrepreneurial sector. As in the case of food security, the development of an entrepreneurial class has long been a strategic priority for Qatar, is a target of its 2030 National Vision, and is central to attempts to diversify the economy away from oil and gas. In his comprehensive survey of the measures taken to boost support mechanisms and incentives for entrepreneurship since the blockade began, Tok demonstrates clearly the unprecedented linkage and awareness that now exist across Qatari society of the importance of entrepreneurship to socio-economic development and growth.

Religion, as Sohaira Z. M. Siddiqui notes, was introduced into the politics of the blockade from the start because it was launched in the middle of the holy month of Ramadan. After assessing the reasons for this decision and its implications, she explores the role of religious arguments and counter-arguments in the crisis. In particular, she examines how religion and religious rhetoric have been used to both justify and undermine the legitimacy of the blockade. In these terms, what has occurred can be viewed as part of a larger process of interaction between religion and the state across the Arab world in general, and the GCC countries in particular.

Jocelyn Sage Mitchell also locates her assessment of the domestic policy opportunities that have been engendered by the blockade in terms of the rapidly changing situation at the GCC level. She argues that the events of the last year have undermined the normal parameters of social, economic and institutional interaction between GCC member states and between different constituencies within those states. This has, in turn, enabled Qatar's rulers to seize the opportunity to implement domestic policy goals that in the past were subject to local and external obstacles. She argues that the upshot of this may, over time, not only reshape Qatar but also the wider Gulf region as a whole.

In the final chapter of section one, Maryah B. Al-Dafa examines the ways in which Qatar Foundation, as the country's leading civil society actor, has responded to the crisis. Over the last year, the universities and research centers under the Foundation's umbrella have served as a focal point for a multifaceted policy and academic debate on the implications and opportunities of the crisis. The Foundation has also played a more practical role in helping staff and students from blockading countries deal with the new challenges they face in staying in Qatar, while facilitating the return to academic life of Qatari students forced to abandon their studies in blockading countries.

As well as serving as the location of two of America's most strategically placed overseas military bases, Qatar is also home to Al Jazeera, one of the world's most influential news networks. In recent decades, it has also emerged as a key player in regional diplomacy and in the global energy, financial, investment and property markets. These considerations, among others, mean that the blockade has a significant international component and, in part, explains why so many members of the international community have called for a peaceful resolution of hostilities that prioritizes a return to regional stability.

In acknowledgement of this, the second section of the volume assesses the blockade in its wider regional and international context. It begins with two chapters that draw on the theoretical literature in International Relations to examine the crisis from the perspective of small state theory and Foreign Policy Analysis (FPA). Rory Miller begins his contribution by noting that the blockade has, among other things, ignited a debate on whether Qatar can counterbalance size-related difficulties to maintain political autonomy, diplomatic influence and economic sovereignty. This, in turn, he argues, has engendered a more general debate over the role and power of small states in the international system. In his analysis, he investigates whether Qatar's handling of this particular crisis provides a suitable case study for other small states facing their own hostile security environments and, if so, what it tells us about small state behavior in international affairs.

In his chapter, Gerd Nonneman considers the causes of the blockade and the reasons why the parties have not yet been able to resolve their differences through the prism of Foreign Policy Analysis (FPA), a sub-discipline of International Relations. In doing so, he examines a wide range of factors – including the role of bureaucracies, the personalities/types of leaders and the patterns of domestic and foreign policymaking. This throws much-needed light on the wide array of often overlapping considerations that have influenced decision-makers in Doha, Abu Dhabi and Riyadh since the crisis began.

We live in an era of cyber threats that have the potential to undermine societal security and prosperity. In the next chapter, Joseph J. Boutros considers the main pillars of cyber security as they relate to sovereign states in general and Qatar in particular. Using available government data, he then analyzes the rising number of reports of electronic crimes in Qatar in the five years before the crisis, as well as the main vulnerabilities of Qatar's internet backbone. Boutros argues that the blockade in itself has had no direct influence on the number of cyber incidents or cyber attacks in Qatar. He does, however, examine the ways that the crisis has influenced thinking on cyber security given that prior to the launch of the blockade hackers took full control of the network belonging to Qatar News Agency (QNA).

The impact of the crisis on future energy cooperation and energy security on the regional and international levels is addressed in the next two chapters. This is an important issue given Qatar's current status as the world's number one exporter of liquefied natural gas (LNG). Steven Wright frames this issue in terms of the major changes in a global gas market increasingly defined by competition, stagnant demand and an oversupply of gas, all of which have resulted in depressed prices. As he shows, prior to the start of the blockade these factors had influenced Qatar to engage more deeply with its neighbors in order to establish itself as a secure and reliable supplier of natural gas across the Gulf. The current stand-off has stalled this, raising challenges for Qatar as a gas supplier and for its long-time regional partners as gas consumers.

Damilola S. Olawuyi agrees with Wright that, in terms of energy cooperation, the current breakdown in relations among GCC states is a lost opportunity for the entire region. He also examines the gas issue from the perspective of international energy law and analyzes how the blockade has undermined the chances of an integrated regional electricity market and a coordinated approach to climate change and low carbon energy transition. At the same time, he argues that the events of the last year have provided Qatar with an opportunity to establish itself as a champion of a more robust multilateral cooperative approach to gas production and supply.

The section on international affairs concludes with Harry Verhoeven's examination of competition between Gulf actors in the critically important African region in light of the crisis. This "other Arab Cold War," as Verhoeven terms it, is a particularly pertinent issue to consider because in June 2017 four African nations cut diplomatic relations with Qatar (Chad, Comoros, Mauritania and Senegal) and three downgraded them (Djibouti, Gabon and Niger). This has significant strategic implications given that the Arab Gulf states are now major actors in Africa and Africa is increasingly vital for Gulf security and prosperity.

The third and final section of the book contains three articles examining the ways in which the crisis has played out in the traditional and social media. Banu Akdenizli's chapter considers the role of Twitter in the first 100 days of the crisis. As she explains, social media is an increasingly important foreign policy instrument, used to craft an online image and communicate messages to large audiences across the world. US President Donald Trump's resort to Twitter in the first days of the crisis is, as Akdenizli notes, a perfect example of this evolving use of social media at the policy level. She then examines in detail the Twitter use of the foreign ministers and foreign ministries of the four Gulf nations embroiled in the crisis and assesses what this says about their strategies, attitudes and engagement with contemporary public diplomacy.

Ashraf Fattah's chapter seeks to shed light on the strategies employed by some journalists writing hard news reports on the Gulf crisis, and how there is often a tendency to turn supposedly objective news into subjective opinion. The case study used by Fattah to assess this form of editorialization of hard news is the special section devoted to coverage of the blockade in the UAE's Arabic daily *Al-Ittihad*. Fattah argues that the news reports included in this study reveal the extent to which supposedly neutral reporting was often more about expressing views than retelling the news.

In the final chapter of the book, Christina Paschyn examines editorials and opinion pieces, as opposed to hard news, published digitally in the first nine months of the blockade by four international outlets – *The Telegraph* and *The Guardian* in the United Kingdom and Fox News and CNN in the United States. Though acknowledging that her findings are not comprehensive, her analysis of the data shows that, over the period examined, commentary in the more conservative media outlets (*The Telegraph* and Fox News) expressed stronger criticism of Qatar and more sympathy for Saudi Arabia on the matter of the legitimacy and necessity of the blockade, while the more liberal outlets (*The Guardian* and CNN) were either more sympathetic to Qatar or presented a more balanced assessment of the crisis.

The short-term goal in putting this volume together has been to draw on the intellectual resources and expertise available in a diverse group of institutions affiliated with Qatar Foundation to document and analyze the first year of the crisis from a number of perspectives and to offer an initial assessment of lessons learned. The longer-term hope is that this volume will serve as a unique and highly informed record of the impact of, and responses to, the blockade in Qatari society, across the wider region and throughout the international community. With these distinct, but overlapping, goals in mind the entire work is complemented by a series of photographs (provided by Suzi Mirgani of the Center for International and Regional Studies (CIRS) at Georgetown University) that offer a rare and unmatched visual chronicle of the dynamics of the first year of the blockade of Qatar.

Rory Miller
Doha, 2018

Section 1:

Economics, Politics and Society

Adapting Ambitions at the Time of Crisis: Qatar's International Cultural Strategies

KAREN EXELL, UNIVERSITY COLLEGE LONDON (UCL) QATAR

The international arts media initially regarded the Gulf crisis as almost wholly detrimental to the cultural activities of a tiny Gulf state that has staked so much on its investments in art and culture as a vehicle for cultural branding, global visibility and geopolitical positioning. For example, on 13 June 2017, eight days into the blockade, *The Art Newspaper* reported that "[t]he diplomatic crisis in the Middle East, which has resulted in the partial blockade of Qatar, is likely to destabilise cultural institutions and partnerships in the region."[1] While intraregional interactions have indeed been limited, Qatar's international cultural projects have continued unchecked and its cultural institutions remain robust. In fact, the blockade has given Qatar a platform to attract attention to its cultural projects whilst using the increased media attention to position itself on the moral high ground by, for example, projecting a positive message regarding its relationship to its foreign resident populations.

On 2 November 2017, Sheikha Al Mayassa bint Hamad bin Khalifa Al Thani, chairperson of Qatar Museums and one of the world's highest profile patrons of the arts, gave the keynote address to the Seventh Hamad bin Khalifa Symposium on Islamic Art, "Islamic Art: Past, Present and Future," held at Virginia Commonwealth University in Richmond, Virginia, whose School of the Arts has a branch in Doha. After listing some of the artists, both international and "contemporary Islamic" as she described them, who

---

1   Gareth Hart and Aimee Dawson, 'Blockade of Qatar threatens cultural institutions,' *The Art Newspaper*, 13 June 2017.

have been hosted by Qatar – Damien Hirst, Cai Guo-Ciang, Richard Serra, Takeshi Murakami, Luc Tuymens, Shirin Neshat, Mona Hatoum, Wael Shawky and Dia Al Azzawi – she stated that:

> the current crisis in the Gulf thus frames any conversation about contemporary culture and by extension arts in the region … Ours is a country made up of diverse populations, over 100 different nationalities live in Qatar. In such a place where many cultures intersect and people cohabit peacefully and in harmony, the value of cultivating an open mind is paramount. Similarly, in the international arena we have always engaged in conversation with the world, and even when our views differed from others we addressed such differences in a respectful and dignified manner. This approach is evident in everything that we do, including our activities relating to contemporary art.[1]

Sheikha Al Mayassa's emphasis on Qatar's approach to inclusivity was evident in the *Contemporary Art Qatar* exhibition in Berlin (Kraftwerk, 9 December 2017 – 3 January 2018), part of the Qatar-Germany Year of Culture,[2] an exhibition which showcased the work of young Qatari artists, both nationals and foreign residents. One of the artists who received a high level of media attention was Emiline Soares, Qatari-born with Portuguese and Indian roots, whose work, "Shifting Identities," consists of an intricate carpet made of colored sand patterns altered by visitors walking on it, reflecting, according to the artist, her experience of the complex, shifting identities of Qatar's population.[3] Reem Al Thani, the exhibition curator, is quoted in Britain's *Guardian* newspaper as saying, "The essence of the

---

1   Available on Youtube at: https://www.youtube.com/watch?v=N70945pPJvk&feature=youtu.be

2   The Year of Culture Program has been running since 2012, with a partnership with Japan in the inaugural year, then with the United Kingdom (2013), Brazil (2014), Turkey (2015), China (2016), and Germany (2017). Future partnerships with India (2019) and France (2020) are in the planning stage. Some years in advance of the blockade, a Year of Culture with Saudi Arabia had been under discussion but did not progress.

3   'Qatar's dynamic young artists showcased in major Berlin exhibition,' *The Guardian*, 10 December 2017.

exhibition is the changing perceptions of Doha, and it's in the nature of our multi-cultural state that I honestly can't tell you who is a Qatari-born artist and who is not; there are all sorts of people represented on the walls here."[1]

In addition to the celebration of diversity, Sheikha Al Mayassa also used her address to reference Qatar's dialogic approach to international diplomatic engagement, an approach contrary to that of the blockading Gulf states of Saudi Arabia, the United Arab Emirates (UAE), Bahrain and their allies, who have avoided direct dialogue throughout the crisis. This keynote address captured Qatar's smart exploitation of the crisis through culture to project a message of moral superiority intended to beneficially alter international perceptions. It is also illuminating as a form of indirect criticism of the members of the anti-Qatar coalition. This use of culture can be contrasted with the recent omission of Qatar from a map of the Gulf in the Louvre Abu Dhabi. This caused an international outcry, and forced the UAE to declare it an error which has since been rectified, though it is of note that it was replaced with a map that removes the demarcation between the Omani territory of Musandam and the UAE.[2]

Qatar's Evolving Cultural Strategy

At the time of writing, eight months into the blockade, Qatar, through one of its key government cultural organizations, Qatar Museums, is hosting two major exhibitions from Germany, *Driven by German Design* (Al Riwaq Gallery, 3 October 2017 – 14 January 2018) curated by the late Martin Roth, and *German Encounters – Contemporary Masterworks from the Deutsche Bank Collection* (Fire Station Artist in Residence, 3 October 2017 – 20 January 2018), counterparts to the contemporary art exhibition in Germany. Other exhibitions in Qatar include the more regionally focused *Imperial Threads: Motifs and Artisans from Turkey, Iran and India* (Museum of Islamic Art, 15 March 2017 – 27 January 2018) – inadvertently outlining newly clarified regional alliances – and *Powder and Damask: Islamic Arms and Armour from the Collection of Fadel Al-Mansoori* (Museum of Islamic Art, 27 August 2017 – 12 May 2018). When the

1 Ibid.
2 'Louvre Abu Dhabi replaces Gulf map that omitted Qatar,' *Gulf Times*, 22 January 2018.

blockade began, on 5 June 2017, two exhibitions represented countries now on opposite sides in the current hostilities: a Turkish collector in *Contemporary Calligraphy – Mehmet Çebi Collection* (Al Riwaq Gallery, 15 May – 17 June 2017), and an Egyptian artist in *Project Space 9: Basim Magdy* (Mathaf: Arab Museum of Modern Art, 15 March – 14 September 2017). This snapshot gives an idea of the range of Qatar's ever-evolving cultural strategy operating at the local, regional and international levels by mid-2017.

Qatar Museums was established in 2005 as Qatar Museums Authority to implement the outward-facing cultural strategy of the then Amir of Qatar, Sheikh Hamad bin Khalifa Al Thani, which formed part of Qatar's robust soft-power diplomatic engagement with Europe and the United States, a strategy essential for defense reasons for a tiny state with fluctuating relationships with its larger regional neighbors. Qatar's investment in Western-style cultural projects at home and its purchase of Western modern and contemporary art have been widely reported. Central to this strategy were high-profile projects such as the Damien Hirst retrospective, *Relics* (Al Riwaq Gallery, 10 October 2013 – 22 January 2014), a version of which took place the previous year at the Tate Modern in London (4 April – 9 September 2012), and the establishment of the Museum of Islamic Art, which opened in Doha in 2008 to much international acclaim.

Although focused on Islamic art, and therefore directly relevant to regional culture, the Museum of Islamic Art can be defined as the first of the new global museums to open in the Arabian Gulf region, housed in a spectacular building designed by the Chinese-American architect, I.M. Pei. Qatar has also invested in establishing itself as the cultural center of the Arab world through regional cultural projects such as Mathaf: Arab Museum of Modern Art, which opened in 2010 with a suite of three exhibitions focusing on modern art production in the Arab world: *Sajjil: A Century of Modern Art* (30 December 2010 – 1 October 2011), *Told/Untold/Retold: 23 Stories of Journeys through Time and Place* and *Interventions: A Dialogue between the Modern and the Contemporary* (both 30 December 2010 – 28 May 2011). Since its inception, Mathaf has programmed exhibitions of Arab and Islamic artists with differing levels of profile, including those mentioned in Sheikha Al Mayassa's keynote address; Mathaf has been described as an expression of Qatar's cultural power resulting in "an Arab space created on Qatar's initiative."[1]

Qatar Museums' most popular project to date in terms of engagement with the Qatari and regional national populations is *Mal Lawal*, an exhibition of private collections that took place in 2012, for Qatari collectors, and in 2014, for collectors from across the Gulf region. A third edition is planned for 2019, potentially at the new National Museum of Qatar, which is scheduled to open in December 2018. Originally intended as a mechanism to gather heritage collections for the National Museum project, the exhibition has been hugely successful in its own right, showcasing the extremely popular practice of private collecting in spaces designed to represent the Qatari *majlis* (a traditional reception room) in 2012 and the natural environment of the Arabian Gulf two years later in 2014.

This second exhibition included a café serving traditional Qatari cuisine that, during the course of the exhibition, became one of Doha's most popular meeting places for nationals. *Mal Lawal* is closely related to the projects coordinated through Qatar's other cultural institutions, including the Ministry of Culture and Katara Cultural Village. These have included heritage activities focused on Qatari and Arabian Gulf traditions aimed at a national audience. Last year, Katara Cultural Village organized regionally significant events such as the Katara International Hunting and Falcons Festival (20–24 September 2017) and the Dhow Festival (14–18 November 2017), the former notable for the participation of falcon organizations from European countries, though representatives from the hostile Gulf states were absent. While the nationalization of traditional cultural activities such as falconry has been a central element of nation-building activities across the region over the last 40 years, festivals celebrating such activities have traditionally attracted participation from across the Gulf states, revealing of the nature of such traditions as simultaneously institutionalized for separatist national purposes whilst representing an element of a *khaleeji*, or Gulf, identity – an identity always imprecise and severely challenged by the crisis that began in June 2017.

---

1   Edward MacDonald-Toone, *Curating the Region: Exhibitions, Geopolitics and the Reception of Contemporary and Modern Art from the Arab World and the Middle East*, Unpublished PhD Thesis, University College London, 2017, p. 151.

Regional exclusions both ways from such activities have become the norm since the blockade began. Qatari participation in cultural festivals in the hostile states are no longer possible. Similarly, Qatar-based speakers were disinvited from the conference "Museums in Arabia," which took place at the Bahrain National Museum in October 2017. On a more global level, there was no official Qatari presence at the opening of the Louvre Abu Dhabi in November 2017, despite Qatar using the same architect, Jean Nouvel, for its own National Museum.

The Rhetoric of Culture

The public statements of Qatar Museums and its Chairperson, Sheikha Al Mayassa, trace the organization's shifting agendas. In 2010 in relation to the Museum of Islamic Art, Sheikha Al Mayassa stated, "[w]e need to respect each other's cultures ... [P]eople in the West don't understand the Middle East. They come with bin Laden in their heads."[1] Takeshi Murakami, whose exhibition *Ego* took place in Qatar in 2012, reflects this viewpoint in a quote still available on the Qatar Museums' website that affirms that Sheikha Al Mayassa "has chosen to use the resources at her disposal to give her people access to the world's best art and to promote intercultural understanding."[2] By 2018 the trope of intercultural dialogue is still present but is balanced by an emphasis on the development of home-grown talent and community engagement, with statements such as, "We provide experiences that motivate local communities, showcase subjects that touch everyday lives, and create the conditions for creativity to flourish in Qatar."[3] Sheikha Al Mayassa is now also quoted as saying, "Qatar Museums is 'local first' in its outlook, investing in the people of Qatar as a priority and extending their horizons. It brings international artists to Qatar and showcases local and regional artists to the world."[4]

The same rhetorical shift is evident in relation to Mathaf, whose early mission statement explained that the project aimed to gather, document,

---

1   Quoted in Nicolai Ouroussoff, 'Building museums and a fresh Arab identity,' *The New York Times*, 26 November 2010.

2   Available at: http://www.qm.org.qa/en/her-excellency-sheikha-al-mayassa

3   Available at: http://www.qm.org.qa/en/area/museums-galleries

4   Available at: http://www.qm.org.qa/en/her-excellency-sheikha-al-mayassa

research and present Arab modern art, bringing it to the attention of the world; by 2018 we read that Mathaf is "a boundary-breaking museum that asks the local community to celebrate the present-day creativity of the Arab world."[1] The shift reflects Qatar Museums' response to a groundswell of criticism that came to a head in 2013 when a Qatari journalist openly criticized Qatar Museums for its perceived preference for foreign, in particular "Western," projects and staff at the expense of Qatari national interests[2] – projects such as *Mal Lawal* were not enough to balance local perceptions of Qatar Museums' priorities.

In response, Qatar Museums has invested in projects that emphasize support for local cultural production, such as the Fire Station Artists in Residence. Opened in 2015, it is tasked with organizing residencies and exhibitions to promote the development of Qatari national and non-national resident artists. While exhibitions of international artists have continued, through the Year of Culture program and collaborations such as the recent *Picasso-Giacometti* exhibition (22 February – 21 May 2017) with the Musée National Picasso and the Fondation Giacometti, the use of the Fire Station as the venue for the latter exhibition indicates an intention to promote as a priority local engagement with the exhibition.

Conclusion and Lessons Learned

The new National Museum of Qatar encompasses the shifting agendas of the last decade and illuminates the ambitions at the heart of the myriad cultural activities that are outlined above. This impressive project was initiated during the reign of the Father Amir, Sheikh Hamad, whose global ambitions are evident in the choice of Jean Nouvel as architect. The project has continued in development during the reign of the more conservative current Amir, Sheikh Tamim bin Hamad Al Thani, and is slated to open 18 months after the start of the blockade in December 2018. In a move calculated for maximum benefit in terms of buttressing and showcasing Qatar's current moral high ground, Sheikh Tamim's first public appearance in

1   Available at: http://www.qm.org.qa/en/project/mathaf-arab-museum-modern-art

2   Faisal Al Marzouki, in *Al Arab* (Arabic), 25 August 2013; English translation, *The Peninsula Qatar*, 26 August 2013.

Qatar after the start of the blockade took place at the National Museum on 20 June 2017, accompanied by a press release that quotes Sheikha Al Mayassa as saying:

> Today marks a proud moment for Qatar as we announce the official opening date for our iconic National Museum [December 2018]. The museum is the physical manifestation of Qatar's proud identity, connecting the country's history with its diverse and cosmopolitan present. It will reflect a part of every Qatari's life, representing our roots and identity. The opening of the National Museum of Qatar will firmly position our country on the global map as a progressive, knowledge-based economy with a long and rich history and give Qatar a voice in the world.[1]

This official royal visit to the National Museum project provided an early platform for Sheikha Al Mayassa to re-emphasize the ongoing use of culture to communicate with the world. This has been a key tenet of Qatar's cultural strategy since the reign of the father amir. Perhaps more significantly, this visit was used as an opportunity to announce the further shift in the country's cultural agenda toward a new definition of the national and the local that revolves around diversity. The positive referencing of diversity in connection with the National Museum of Qatar implies that this museum may establish an important precedent in how the nation is represented in museums region-ally. This is a noticeable break with the way that national museums across the region presented an exclusive nationals-only identity during the early phase of regional independence in the late 1960s and 1970s – though, admittedly, this omission of any acknowledgement of foreign contributions to the nation's history was arguably a necessity for emergent and fragile nations.[2]

A number of regional cultural interactions have been restricted as a

---

1   Quoted on, for example, the local information website *Marhaba*, 'HH The Emir of Qatar visits the National Museum site,' https://www.marhaba.qa/hh-the-emir-of-qatar-visits-the-national-museum-of-qatar-site/

2   See for example, Karen Exell, *Modernity and the Museum in the Arabian Peninsula*, Abingdon: Routledge, 2016; John Thabiti Willis, 'A Visible Silence: Africans in the History of Pearl Diving in Dubai, UAE', in Karen Exell and Sarina Wakefield (eds.), *Museums in Arabia: Transnational Practices and Regional Processes*, Abingdon: Routledge, 2016, pp. 34–50.

consequence of the current crisis. There have also been resource impacts in the cultural sector as some citizens from blockading nations working on Qatar-based projects have had to return home. International cultural consultancies with projects on both sides of the conflict have also found it increasingly difficult to manage and navigate the complexities and challenges of the ongoing stand-off. However, early predictions that the blockade would have a wholly negative impact on Qatar's cultural activities have not become a reality.

As Sheikh Saoud bin Abdulrahman Al Thani, Qatar's ambassador to Germany, stated in relation to the *Contemporary Art Qatar* exhibition in Berlin, "In some ways, [the blockade] has helped us to showcase our art ... A lot of journalists have travelled to Doha and, of course, when they are there, they are not only reporting about the blockade, but also about the culture."[1] Qatar has so far succeeded in making tactical use of this unplanned media attention. It has capitalized on its position as underdog to win international sympathy and project a utopian moral message of inclusivity through the platform of culture. In doing so, it has not only reinforced its existing reputation for political agility and smart diplomacy but has also promoted its cultural and creative sector before a global audience.

---

1   Catherine Hickley, 'Qatar brings desert sands to snowy Berlin,' *The Art Newspaper*, 11 December 2017.

Food Security: The Case of Qatar

TAREQ AL-ANSARI, HAMAD BIN KHALIFA UNIVERSITY

The security and sustainability of energy, water and food resources are of increasing importance, and feature as a priority issue in most international forums alongside climate change and other major challenges facing the modern world. The global population is growing, expected to reach 9 billion by 2050, increasing demand for resources and, in line with this, global food production will need to increase by 50% to 100% in order to feed the expanding population.[1] This requires actors across the entire international system to collectively expand food production, and to do so whilst considering multiple external stressors such as climate change. Modern, global food systems comprised of a complex set of activities ranging from production through to consumption are required to respond to these challenges.

A typical modern food system has multiple moving parts, inherently interconnected at different dimensions (economic, social and environmental), and scales (temporal and spatial). Food systems have evolved from primitive systems to multifaceted structures with integrated supply chains. An ideal food system maximizes benefits for all and contributes to food security. Responding to global challenges and uncertainties, food systems are required to demonstrate: productivity and efficiency in resource utilization; responsiveness to changing demands; environmental responsibility; economic competence; and a holistic and resilient approach in design and operation. Qatar's food system is evolving in light of these factors as it faces

---

[1] 'Reaping the Benefits: Science and the Sustainable Intensification of Global Agriculture,' Report of the Royal Society, London, 2009, https://royalsociety.org/topics-policy/publications/2009/reaping-benefits/

multiple challenges, including sudden increases in food prices, supply chain disruptions and environmental challenges. This chapter will consider one component of both the food system and security, which is related to the "availability" of food. It will do so in the context of recent geopolitical events.

As a peninsula on the Arabian Gulf, Qatar's only land border is with Saudi Arabia at Abu Samra in the south. Early on the morning of 5 June 2017, supply chains through Abu Samra serving Qatar were abruptly disrupted, ending the transfer of products, services and people. Air and sea transportation trade routes were also impacted immediately as air space and sea channels controlled by neighboring members of the anti-Qatar coalition were closed off. The circumstances surrounding these events exposed vulnerabilities that any nation importing a majority of its food requirements from international food markets would have experienced in similar circumstances. Nevertheless, the embargo presented a golden opportunity for a multi-scale and multi-dimensional transformation in a Qatari national food system heavily reliant on the global market for its domestic food supply.

The smooth and uninterrupted flow of international trade, with products, commodities and even services moving seamlessly across boundaries, is essential to global stability. Energy and food, including its virtual water constituents (i.e. embodied water), are prime drivers of global supply chains and are resources that are key for human survival and comfort. However, international supply chains are vulnerable to disruption, either through economic or physical drivers such as geopolitical risks and conflict.

Geography is also a relevant factor. Qatar is located within the Arabian Gulf, a shallow semi-enclosed marginal sea with one of the highest recorded salinities in the world, connected to the Gulf of Oman via the narrow Strait of Hormuz. From a global perspective, the region is most recognized for its supply of hydrocarbons to the global energy markets. Whilst Qatar is blessed with an abundance of energy reserves, making it the world's largest exporter of liquified natural gas (LNG), its utilization of fresh water from aquifers far surpasses natural renewal rates. It depends on energy-intensive desalination to cater to its municipal requirements. In terms of resources, there is an inherent interdependency that exists between energy, water and food, known as the EWF nexus. The responsible management of the EWF nexus in an integrated manner is imperative for sustainable development and for the security of supply of all resources.

Qatar's hyper arid environment, combined with its resource characteristics and level of economic development, meant that self-sufficiency prior to the embargo hovered at approximately 12% for vegetables, 49% for meat, 28% for fish, 11% for fruits and dates, 13% for eggs and 0.3% for cereals.[1] The country had little choice but to rely on global markets to satisfy its remaining domestic food requirements, importing approximately 90% of its domestic consumption, the majority through the Abu Samra border crossing. This border not only transmitted food products from Saudi Arabia, but also served as a key transit hub for multiple countries exporting a variety of food groups such as poultry and eggs, milk and other dairy, fruits and vegetables, and edible oils to Qatar.

Food Security

Food security is not a privilege; it is a basic human right, but the question of food security is a pressing global concern. In an ideal world, resources are conserved, consumption is sustained, and food is available to all. The World Food Summit of 1996 states that food security exists when "all people, at all times, have physical, social and economic access to sufficient, safe and nutritious food which meets their dietary needs and food preferences for an active and healthy life."[2] There are three core determinants of food security: (1) food availability, which refers to the amount, type and quality of food a unit has at its disposal to consume; (2) food accessibility, which considers the economic and logistical access to food of those at the household level; and (3) food utilization, which relates to how the food consumed translates into beneficial nutrient intake.

An underdeveloped national food system operating within an environment that is not naturally conducive to farming explains Qatar's dependence on global markets for its food supply. Through a private sector-driven import network, Qatar has depended on trans-boundary supply chains to

---

1   'Aggregate Supply and Consumption Economic Statistics: Agricultural,' Qatar Ministry of Development Planning and Statistics (QMDPS), 2016, https://www.mdps.gov.qa/en/statistics/Statistical%20Releases/Economic/Agriculture/2016/1_Agricuitural_2016_AE.pdf

2   'The Rome Declaration on World Food Security and World Food Summit Plan of Action,' The Food and Agriculture Organization of the United Nations, 1996, http://www.fao.org/docrep/003/w3613e/w3613e00.htm.

meet its domestic requirements. Typically, when relying on global resource markets, whether it is for energy or food, vulnerability to price fluctuations is a plausible scenario. Multiple factors can affect food prices: energy prices, subsidies, demand for biofuels and production trends. In a situation of extreme price fluctuations as witnessed in 2008, Qatar was able to weather a high annual food bill due to its financial resources, especially as oil prices were at near record levels during the same period.

Traditionally, Qatar has ensured the availability of food, including access to a wide range of food products, to satisfy the daily nutritional needs of the population. The notion of availability within the food security context implies that food will be available to all persons at all times, implying that the physical availability of food is indeed a precursor to this. In this regard, there is little or no guidance as to the source of the food. It is important to acknowledge the benefits of globalization in relation to the movement and trade of food products into Qatar, as well as in all other countries where water is scarce and climates are severe. In particular, globalization enables the movement of water as part of the food trade in a concept known as virtual water.[1]

The notion of virtual water is associated with the water consumed during the production of crops that are moved as part of global supply chains. The ideal working of the virtual water concept entails importing water from water-rich regions at a more efficient crop water productivity than would have been achieved by the importing nation. Global virtual water trends and movements of food products are exemplified by water-rich regions exporting food products to countries suffering from physical water scarcity, rather than economic water scarcity. In terms of meeting its domestic food requirements, Qatar has benefited from elements of the virtual water concept by importing from the global market.

That said, the key question is whether food security can be truly attained if the source of the food is not domestic. There are inherent similarities that exist between food security and other kinds of sovereignty.[2] In food security

1   Tony Allan, 'Virtual Water: A Long-Term Solution for Water Short Middle Eastern Economies?,' Paper presented at the 1997 British Association Festival of Science, University of Leeds, Water and Development Session, 9 September 1997, https://www.soas.ac.uk/water/publications/papers/file38347.pdf

2   Such as political sovereignty and economic sovereignty. See Brian Girvin, 'Nationalism, economic growth and political sovereignty,' *The History of European Ideas*, Vol. 15, Nos. 1-3 (August 1992), pp. 177–184.

discussions, it is important to acknowledge that the two concepts exist and that they are neither antagonistic nor conflictive toward one another.[1] However, the main difference is that food sovereignty underscores the promotion of local food systems, primarily small scale and non-industrial in nature with an emphasis on organic and a production system that is nondestructive, environmentally friendly and sustainable in line with principles of agro-ecology.

Food security and sovereignty both: (1) emphasize the need to increase food production; (2) stress that the central problem today is access to food; (3) emphasize the importance of nutrition; and (4) advance social protection.[2] As defined by the United Nations' Food and Agriculture Organization (FAO), food security only considers the availability of food, without considering the location and method of production. Manifesting from food security, the 2007 Nyéléni Declaration established six pillars of food sovereignty: (1) a focus on food for the people; (2) value food providers; (3) localization of the food system; (4) placing control at the local level; (5) development and promotion of knowledge and skills; and (6) work with nature to maximize the contribution of ecosystems, improve resilience and adopt sustainable production methods.[3]

Resilience

Security and resilience are not mutually exclusive. In fact, a strong bond exists between the two. Security can be achieved through resilience against potential harm (or otherwise coercive change) from external forces.[4] The notion of security is manifest in all energy, water and food resources. In the context of food security, although the State of Qatar has the economic strength to provide food to its inhabitants, was it ever really food secure?

Further investigation in this regard requires insight into the factors that

---

1   Gustavo Gordillo and Obed Jeronimo, 'Food Security and Food Sovereignty: Base Documents for Discussion,' Food and Agriculture Organization of the United Nations, 2013, www.fao.org/3/a-ax736e.pdf

2   Ibid.

3   'The Six Pillars of Food Sovereignty, Developed at Nyéléni, 2007,' Food Secure Canada, 2012, http://usc-canada.org/UserFiles/File/SixPillars_Nyeleni.pdf.

4   See Emma Rothschild, 'What Is Security?', Daedalus, Vol. 124, No. 3, The Quest for World Order (Summer, 1995), pp. 53–98.

promote security, notably resilience, as well as the potential disruptors, most importantly existing vulnerabilities. Vulnerability is defined as the degree to which a system or subsystem is likely to experience harm due to exposure to a hazard, either as a perturbation or stressor.[1] A particular system vulnerability is likely to expose the absence of resilience. From a systems perspective this can be expressed as the ability to withstand stresses and shocks and maintain or return to continuity in the event that such shocks or disruptions occur. At times of steady state, there is perhaps little or no impetus to deviate from the norm. However, unforeseen events disrupt systems that are vulnerable. Trans-boundary supply chains are subject to a multitude of disruptors, the most extreme cases being those in which products are prevented from moving beyond their source.

Vulnerability can be deciphered into three dimensions[2] and applied to the traditional Qatar food system, i.e. a system that was dependent on the global market: (1) exposure: related to the reliance on an external source of food products; (2) sensitivity: the degree of reliance versus self-sufficiency; and (3) adaptive capacity: aligned with resilience, this examines the time required to return to a steady state after a disruption has occurred.

Generally, as in the case of Qatar, exposure to a supply chain disruption can occur via either a source or a route disruption and, in extreme cases, both types can occur concurrently. One example of a disruption at source occurred in 2008, with the import ban on all poultry from Saudi Arabia (Qatar's main poultry supplier at the time) due to a suspected outbreak of bird flu, which caused the domestic price of eggs to double in quick time. In 2017, in another example, Qatar halted meat imports from Brazil due to other health and safety concerns.

The Transformation

The launch of the embargo in June 2017 will forever be viewed as a turning point for Qatar's food system. One immediate consequence of the crisis was that it served to underscore that while participation in global trade is both

---

1 Bille L. Turner, et al, 'A Framework for Vulnerability Analysis in Sustainability Science,' *Proceedings of National Academy of Science*, Vol. 100, No. 14 (June 2003), pp. 8074–9.

2 Ibid.

unavoidable and important, security of resource supply is also necessary. It also raised the question, from a food security perspective, of what constitutes security. Is it a level of domestic self-sufficiency? A diversity of supply chains? Or an investment in strategic reserves? The optimal answer to these questions most likely includes all three working together in a way that makes them dynamic and resilient in their operation and sustainable in their nature. This includes storing long-life food products, enhancing self-sufficiency with economically viable crops, and importing crops, such as cereals, that cannot be grown efficiently locally.

Furthermore, to what extent can principles of food sovereignty influence and share the transformation narrative in Qatar? Plans to upgrade the domestic food system in terms of self-sufficiency began long before the start of the June 2017 crisis. For instance, the Hassad Food company, a subsidiary of the Qatar Investment Authority (QIA), has been strategically investing for more than a decade in key agri-markets, including Australia, where annual output from its farming interests is 130,000 tons of grain, and 160,000 head of sheep.[1]

Similarly, the onset of the 2008 food price rise was the main impetus for the initiation of the Qatar National Food Security Program. It has a dual mandate: to highlight all the potential risks to the availability of food in Qatar and to develop a comprehensive food security strategy that addresses these risks. The program has also taken into account sustainability principles, market reform and a food supply strategy consisting of strategic reserves, enhanced domestic production for selected crops (fresh and perishable) and a diversified supply chain network to import selected crops, especially those demanding a large water requirement. In addition, in 2013, Qatar was a founding member of the Dry Land Alliance, which is headquartered in Doha. Its mandate is to align countries facing similar challenges in terms of dry land agriculture.

In these terms, the crisis that began in June 2017 only served to cement the need for translating the existing food security narrative into concrete action on the ground. As a consequence, respective food security plans have now been accelerated.

---

1   Hassad Australia is a fully owned subsidiary of Hassad Food. It was established in 2009 and currently owns nine farms across three Australian states, spanning a total land area of more than 152,000 hectares, http://www.hassad.com/English/Pages/Hassad-Australia.aspx

Hamad Port, a national asset, was crucial in minimizing any disruption of supply post-June 2017. The port began operations in December 2016, and was officially inaugurated in September 2017, following the start of the embargo. In its first year, it could claim 22 direct shipping routes between Hamad Port and several regional and international seaports and approximately 120 navigation destinations. In line with this, its capacity increased rapidly during its first 14 months, reaching the one million TEU (twenty-foot equivalent unit) mark.[1] In July 2017, Qatar announced plans to build a food storage and processing facility at Hamad Port, capable of stockpiling three main commodities – rice, sugar and edible oils – for three million people for two and a half years.[2]

In the immediate aftermath of the food supply chain disruption, the Hassad Food company also supplied the local market with a range of strategic products (eggs, poultry, and fresh fruits and vegetables) from at least 10 different countries including Turkey, Kuwait, Azerbaijan, Oman and Lebanon. Moreover, in conjunction with Hassad Australia and Widam Food, 340,000 head of Australian sheep (chilled carcasses) were delivered to Qatar over the first three months of the embargo.[3]

Above and beyond such moves, going forward, and as part of the long-term strategy for domestic agriculture, it is necessary to undertake the type of development that involves the upgrade of domestic infrastructure in order to enhance productivity and ensure a continuous and resource-efficient food production system throughout the year. In this regard, and in quick succession, both commercial and hobby farms have increased their production capacity and supply to the local market. Government entities such as the Ministry of Municipality and Environment, the Ministry of Economy and Commerce, the Qatar Development Bank (QDB) and Hassad Food are driving various initiatives to support the private sector across a wide range of small-, medium- and large-scale projects in all food groups.

For instance, the government has recently supported and overseen a number of private sector, large-scale projects in the areas of poultry, fish

---

1 'Hamad Port reaches 1mn TEU milestone in record time,' *Gulf Times*, 19 March 2018.

2 'Qatar to build food storage, processing plant at Hamad Port,' *Gulf Times*, 16 July 2017.

3 'Qatar steps up efforts to achieve food security,' *Qatar Tribune*, 19 July 2017.

and alfalfa. The poultry project is the largest domestic poultry project to date and upon completion it will have a production capacity of 70,000 tons of broiler meat and 250 million eggs per year, enough to cover current and future market demand.[1] Many more projects in other food groups, including fruits and vegetables, are also planned.

For its part, QDB has supported, and continues to support, various agriculture schemes through very attractive financing mechanisms. It has also recently launched the "green house program," which consists of technical and financial mechanisms aimed at boosting production at household level by encouraging home owners to grow their own food. Likewise, Hassad Food has recently launched an initiative to help local farmers increase productivity. The *IKTEFA* program targets the estimated 80% of Qatari farms that are currently unproductive.[2]

In what is almost a complete sectoral transformation, Qatar has also moved from being almost entirely dependent on the global market for its meat and dairy requirements. Both the public and private sector have been instrumental in alleviating the intended effects of the supply chain disruption on both products. The government, for example, moved swiftly to facilitate the substitution of dairy products previously sourced from Saudi Arabia. Within days, a range of international alternatives, notably from suppliers in Turkey, were available on supermarket shelves. The private sector was also very responsive. In one case that gained the interest of the international media, a local businessman imported 3,400 cows by air in order to provide a local source of milk and other dairy products as part of his contribution to offsetting the negative consequences of the embargo.

These steps were necessary to ensure the availability of food in the short to medium term. However, the overarching longer-term goal must be to go even further to achieve higher levels of, if not complete, self-sufficiency. Incidentally, the Baladna dairy company has effectively created a dairy industry in Qatar since the launch of the embargo and has announced that it aims to increase the number of cows in Qatar to at least 10,000, in order to raise its production of fresh milk and yoghurt to 500 tons a day. This is

1   'Al Rayan plans largest poultry farm in Qatar,' *Qatar Tribune*, 1 October 2017.
2   'Qatar steps up efforts to achieve food security,' *Qatar Tribune*, 19 July 2017.

enough to meet 100% of domestic demand for those products and also create an export capacity of 100 tons.[1]

Conclusion and Lessons Learned

Achieving the national food security/sovereignty aspirations of the State of Qatar can have dual benefits. It can enhance domestic self-sufficiency, at the same time contributing to the global drive for increased food production. The challenge for Qatar, as well as all other food producers, is how to increase food production within a sustainable development framework. This sustainable intensification, as it is known, basically refers to a process whereby the current generation can deliver increased levels of nutritious food without impacting on the capacity of future generations to do the same.

Sustainable development alongside food security/sovereignty are critical to the development and continued transformation of Qatar's food system. From an EWF nexus perspective, Qatar must effectively take advantage of its massive gas reserves and its sunshine, as a potential for solar energy utilization, as ways to offset the challenges it faces in growing food efficiently as a result of its natural environment.

System characteristics such as resilience and sustainability can exist in isolation. However, a system that is both sustainable and resilient is certainly desirable and while designing such a system is challenging, the evolving Qatari national food system should aspire to achieve both. If it can do so, then Qatar can become a leading player in dry land agriculture and even a model of food system efficiency, with sound economic and social policies operating within an environmentally responsible development framework.

Today, significant efforts to overhaul the food system are evident and levels of self-sufficiency are progressively rising with the emphasis on productivity improvements and a reduction in water consumption. Latest reports indicate that since the embargo began, self-sufficiency levels have increased to 24% for fruits and vegetables, 50% for animal crops, and 82%

---

1   'Qatari dairy company Baladna to go public next year: Sources,' *The Peninsula Qatar*, 15 December 2017.

for dairy products. In the future, Qatar will strive to achieve the following levels of self-sufficiency:[1]

- 70% in fresh vegetables within two years;
- 100% in dairy within eight months;
- 90% in eggs within two years;
- 100% in fish and shrimp within two years.

In conclusion, although the security of food supply is the objective of the food security narrative, an integrated resource approach is both desirable and necessary for sustainable development and for ensuring the security of EWF resources. This is because expanding local production is directly linked to the sustainable use of energy and water resources. As such, an EWF nexus approach for the sustainable intensification of food production in Qatar as part of the food security narrative is a plausible way to design a highly resource-efficient food system.

There was never a question of *if* Qatar should increase its domestic production. The real question has always been *how* Qatar can develop an exemplary holistic food system for dry land agriculture which is robust, efficient, sustainable, secure and resilient so that it ensures that food is available to all and at all times. One important consequence of the embargo has been that this question has now been elevated to the top of the economic, development and national security agenda.

---

1   'Qatar is self-sufficient in vegetables in two years... and milk in 8 months,' *Al-Arab*, 20 April 2018.

Entrepreneurship in Qatar:
Is the Blockade a Golden Opportunity?

M. EVREN TOK, HAMAD BIN KHALIFA UNIVERSITY

Under the Qatar National Vision 2030 (QNV), Qatar aims to diversify its economy from its overreliance on extractive resources. Entrepreneurship development, and especially the development of small and medium enterprises, is an important strategic economic tool intended to contribute to the implementation of this vision. In order to do this, the government has adopted a proactive approach that encourages, in various ways, entrepreneurship development. Collaborations between the public and private sectors and the creation of specific organizations to finance and support new enterprises and to expand entrepreneurship education in the country have also played an important complementary role alongside policymaking.

Given that these various approaches have evolved over the last decade or more, it would be unfair to argue that Qatar's drive and commitment to stimulate entrepreneurship began with the blockade; however, the blockade triggered a multitude of forces and dynamics that converged to develop entrepreneurship. The crisis engendered by the blockade made even more explicit and pressing the need to reduce Qatari dependence in strategic sectors such as food. Increased independence and self-sufficiency come with the capacity to produce a wide variety of goods and services domestically. This is one way in which entrepreneurship may play an important role in post-blockade Qatar. The crisis may also contribute to fostering innovation in critical sectors, which will make Qatari businesses more competitive in the global market over the longer term.

Is the blockade a golden opportunity? The immediate answer to the question is "yes" – the blockade led to the identification of new opportunities in terms of trade routes, strategies, markets and networks. Nevertheless, the blockade is a golden opportunity for Qatar not only because it has replaced old networks and modalities with new ones or led to alternative revenue generation streams or trade routes. Rather, it is a golden opportunity because Qatar's entrepreneurship ecosystem[1] has been reflecting communitarian responses to the blockade and manifesting socially and culturally embedded economic actions. In other words, Qatari society as a whole has reacted against the blockade in economic terms, and in this environment and context entrepreneurship is critical.

This chapter will examine these emerging social forces that encourage entrepreneurship development. It will also address the wider issue of entrepreneurship in Qatar by examining some of its fundamentals, and highlight Qatar's international and national performance in promoting entrepreneurial endeavors. The major actors in Qatar's entrepreneurship ecosystem will be introduced, together with their roles and actions. The chapter will then focus on how social forces started to form communitarian reactions to the blockade, which have significant implications for entrepreneurship. The chapter will conclude by providing some lessons learned.

Entrepreneurship in Qatar: The Big Picture

According to the Global Entrepreneurship Network's *Global Entrepreneurship Index 2018*, Qatar ranks 22nd in the world and second in the Middle East and North Africa (MENA) region after Israel. This places Qatar at the head of the Gulf Cooperation Council (GCC) countries when it comes to entrepreneurship. According to the same index, in 2016, Qatar ranked 24th in the world.[2] These rankings explicitly show that Qatar has progressed in building a vibrant entrepreneurial system in recent years. As the index points out, this progress is especially notable for the cultural and social support given to entrepreneurship across wider society, an existing condition that was enhanced with the onset of the blockade.

---

1   The entrepreneurship ecosystem is the social and economic environment in which entrepreneurship functions. It includes a variety of stakeholders, serving together and in various ways as an enabling environment.

2   *Global Entrepreneurship Index*, Global Entrepreneurship Development Institute, 2018, https://thegedi.org/global-entrepreneurship-and-development-index/.

Entrepreneurship in Qatar has always been intended to contribute to the diversification of the country's economy in order to reduce its long-term dependency on hydrocarbon income. Related to this has been the goal of establishing a "green" and sustainable model of development. In the pursuit of both, and as part of the wider goal of transitioning to a knowledge-based economy, the Qatari state has placed considerable emphasis on establishing and nurturing an enabling environment for entrepreneurship through generous financial, legal and logistical support.

It should be noted that in addition to direct government efforts, the Qatar National Research Fund (QNRF), a semi-private entity, has been vocal and pro-active about the importance of entrepreneurship. On 29–31 March 2016, in a workshop funded by QNRF and organized by the Haute Ecole de Commerce (HEC) of Paris, entitled "Entrepreneurship 2020," QNRF's Director of Programs, Noor Al Merekhi, explained that entrepreneurship had a critical and central role to play in building Qatar's knowledge-based economy.[1]

In 2012, a Gallup-Silatech joint publication identified "Qatar's rising entrepreneurial spirit."[2] In subsequent years, this spirit has been promoted across the Qatari media. Two years later, in 2014, the Global Entrepreneurship Monitor (GEM) Qatar Report surveyed over 4,000 people – with equal weight given to Qataris and non-Qatari residents.[3] The report revealed that, unlike other innovation-driven economies around the world, social values and culture are some of the drivers fostering entrepreneurship in Qatar. The Silatech Index, which is a nationally representative, semi-annual poll of residents aged between 15 and 29 throughout the Arab world, shows that while entrepreneurial activities among youth in other regional states has been falling, entrepreneurship levels among Qatari youth increased from 24% in 2009 to 33% by the fall of 2011.

This growth, outlined in the report titled "Qatar's Rising Entrepreneurial Spirit," has been stimulated by multiple factors such as: adequate access to funds for youth aged between 15 and 29; knowledge and ease in obtaining loans; and help with legal and other bureaucratic formalities. In a study

---

1   See Qatar National Research Fund, 2016, https://www.qnrf.org.
2   *Qatar's Rising Entrepreneurial Spirit*, Gallup, 2016.
3   *GEM Global Entrepreneurship Monitor*, 2018, http://www.gemconsortium.org/country-profile/102

conducted by the Oxford Consultancy Group, titled "Qatar Employment Report: Insights for 2016", over 300 Qataris between the ages of 16 and 25 were asked about their ideal job.[1] The survey results indicated that 41% of the respondents preferred to run their own business.

Similarly, a more recent report by the Oxford Business Group on entrepreneurship and the establishment of start-ups in 73 countries indicated that 16% of adults in Doha have already participated in entrepreneurial initiatives, while another 50% intend to launch a new business venture within the next three years, all part of a forward-looking vision intended to help Qatar establish itself as a country with the highest level of entrepreneurial ambition and a well-developed ecosystem.[2]

These reports and studies illustrate that among Qataris of all ages there exists great enthusiasm for pursuing entrepreneurial paths and that most individuals feel they are well supported by the state in attempting to achieve their professional dreams. However, entrepreneurship education has yet to address the complexity and vibrancy of the growing entrepreneurship ecosystem of the country. Despite the growing number of specialized training programs for aspiring and new entrepreneurs in local and international universities in Qatar, and the proliferation of institutions and organizations engaged in entrepreneurship education, the country has human capital gaps in key areas for entrepreneurs.

Qatar's Entrepreneurship Ecosystem

In 2015, the World Innovation Summit for Education (WISE) and Qatar University jointly published a report titled "Entrepreneurship Education: A Global Consideration from Practice to Policy Around the World." Authored by leading experts in education policy and entrepreneurship, it argued that the goals of entrepreneurship education vary depending on the necessities of local economies and communities. For its part, the GEM considers entrepreneurial skills developed through government-initiated entrepreneurship programs and entrepreneurship education in schools and at university level as key to entrepreneurial success across society.

---

1   'Qatar employment report,' *Gulf Times*, 2 September 2016.
2   *Qatar Supports Entrepreneurs and Start-Ups*, Oxford: Oxford Business Group, 2018.

Therefore, the identification of local economic circumstances and necessities is vital in scaffolding entrepreneurship ecosystems. In a complementary way, the World Economic Forum (WEF) introduced a framework for an entrepreneurship ecosystem, which stresses that the components of an ecosystem are comprised of universities and support systems within relevant industries such as mentorships, incubators and accelerators. It has also argued that education and training at school are key to achieving a competitive entrepreneurship ecosystem. Overall, as shown in Figure 1, there is a multiplicity of actors and factors that contribute to the development of a viable and successful entrepreneurship ecosystem.

Figure 1 – Constituents of an Entrepreneurship Ecosystem

As part of the Qatar National Vision 2030, the government has been working to create a vibrant entrepreneurship ecosystem. In line with this goal, Enterprise Qatar was established to provide small and medium enterprises (SMEs) with the necessary support, including specialized education. In 2014, Enterprise Qatar was merged with the Qatar Development Bank (QDB), to avoid any overlap in duties and functions and in order to create a more streamlined effort to foster entrepreneurship in the country. A considerable number of private institutions and non-governmental organizations (NGOs) have also been set up to provide entrepreneurship education for young and established entrepreneurs. They include:

- Qatar Development Bank – the largest financial entity, set up by an Amiri Decree to support SMEs in Qatar. It provides support to entrepreneurs in starting up businesses and it offers various financial products.
- INJAZ Qatar – the largest educational partnering organization of local business communities in Qatar. It provides entrepreneurship education programs and services, and programs in preparatory schools, high schools, universities and at youth centers across the country.
- Qatar Business Incubation Center – focuses on incubation and helps entrepreneurs in various ways to start up their business. It provides supplementary services and is focused on addressing obstacles that limit the growth and survival of initiatives in the market place over the longer term.
- Qatar Finance and Business Academy – aspires to raise the quality of the business environment in Qatar by offering various tailored programs to individuals and organizations.
- Qatar Chamber – supports Qatari business interests and opportunities. It is a central organization in terms of information and data regarding the Qatari business community.
- Silatech – promotes job creation and economic opportunities in the MENA region. As a regional organization, it emphasizes innovative enterprise development. It has an extremely large network of organizations in the Arab world and makes an important contribution to the communication and dissemination of research findings to large audiences across the Arab world.
- Nama – promotes social entrepreneurship and innovation.
- Bedaya – a subsidiary of Qatar Development Bank that supports Qatari youth through mentoring and entrepreneurial coaching.
- Qatar University – offers various courses, delivered by the College of Engineering and the College of Business and Economics, introducing students to entrepreneurship and helping develop their entrepreneurial skills. In 2013, the university also launched the Centre for Entrepreneurship, targeting students, alumni, members of various associations, government agencies, and the private sector.
- Carnegie Mellon University in Qatar – in collaboration with the

AlFaisal Without Borders Foundation, launched the AlFaisal-Carnegie Mellon Innovation Entrepreneurship Center.

Qatar Under Siege: The Place of Entrepreneurship in Societal Responses

Entrepreneurship is an embedded and complex process, and consequently being able to bring "context" to entrepreneurship is crucial. In these terms, it is vital to align entrepreneurship with social needs and desires and to provide entrepreneurs with the proper tools to succeed in the specific environment in which they function. Although an entrepreneur is inherently an individual, the entrepreneurial paths that can be followed involve forms of sociality, spatiality and community ties, as well as the various unique conventions, codes and symbols that a localized culture reflects and embraces, including in economic activities. This conceptual perspective is what needs to be emphasized in any analysis of Qatar's reaction to the blockade, an event that invites us to look more closely at the nexus between entrepreneurship, behaviors and the experiences of entrepreneurs, and the moral basis of a society (the impact of cultural traits, norms and values).

One notable individual response came from Eman Al Sulaiti, an experienced entrepreneur. In response to the crisis, she announced that she would support the local community and economy by providing free consultancy services to Qatari nationals aspiring to launch startups. As she explained in a newspaper article on her efforts, this included her helping young entrepreneurs to make the "right connections with suitable dealers, supervisors and corporations," as well as coaching and mentoring.[1] Likewise, Ayhsha Al Mudhahka, CEO of the Qatar Business Incubation Center, acknowledged that "the blockade is a big eye-opener," but one that had served to help "identify the local talent and promote entrepreneurship skills."[2]

The Hamad Bin Khalifa University (HBKU) initiative known by the name HBKU Souqna, has attempted to bring students together with local entrepreneurs to form connections within the local community. It is first and foremost a unique community-university partnership, aspiring to raise

---

1   'Lending a helping hand to budding Qatari entrepreneurs,' *The Peninsula Qatar*, 17 October 2017.

2   Ibid.

awareness of local models of entrepreneurship and economic production that are crucial for diversifying away from the hydrocarbon-based economy. Souqna also serves as a platform to enhance social engagement between the community within Education City and the general public, which allows students to learn more about entrepreneurship from local business owners.

A different version of HBKU's Souqna is a more recent initiative named the Torba Farmers Market. Located at Qatar Foundation's Ceremonial Court in Education City, it brings together local entrepreneurs and small businesses to sell their products, and in the process provides the wider community with homegrown local fruits, vegetables and other agricultural products. One of the tenants in the Torba Farmers Market, Noor Ahmed Al-Ansari, expressed the communitarian nature of emerging forms of entrepreneurship in an eloquent way. "I'm all for promoting local products," she explained, before adding, "… the blockade has actually worked for us. Now a lot of people are encouraging Qatari-based businesses and even home-based businesses."[1]

To harness this enthusiasm and to help those who want to embrace the growing opportunity to engage in entrepreneurship, Qatar University's "Qatar blockade" program offers various supportive initiatives that demonstrate a practical relevance to society, as well as academic and policy-relevant perspectives, that work as a catalyst for the sustainable socio-economic development of Qatar.[2]

Conclusion and Lessons Learned

Qatar's entrepreneurship ecosystem has long provided support for aspiring and established entrepreneurs through a wide range of organizations, institutions, programs, funds, consultations, incubators, loans, degrees and awards. Nevertheless, the blockade has made it more relevant and necessary than ever to ask how this provision can be enhanced, and how remaining gaps in support to entrepreneurs can be identified and filled. Perhaps most importantly, the current crisis demands that we investigate the best ways to

---

1   'Organic, homemade products businesses thrive at Torba Farmers Market,' *Gulf Times*, 24 November 2017.

2   Qatar Blockade Program, Qatar University, http://www.qu.edu.qa/about/qatar-blockade

achieve further learning and to improve synchronization among various entrepreneurship-education providers.

Developments thus far suggest that further encouraging entrepreneurship promotion and relevant education will stimulate the mindsets and skills of budding entrepreneurs in society. No less important is making citizens and residents aware not only of the benefits that entrepreneurial endeavor offers, but also the real opportunities that exist, including new ones that have emerged in direct response to the blockade. Undoubtedly, there is a growing interest in entrepreneurship in the current climate and this can act as a catalyst for socio-economic development and growth and lead to long-term transformations. It is also clear that the inter-connectedness between the communitarian aspects of entrepreneurship and the efforts in recent years to cultivate a more powerful and dynamic enabling environment for entrepreneurship have become more visible and have started to pay real dividends since the anti-Qatar blockade was launched in the summer of 2017.

This demands that new opportunities for community-based entrepreneurship be explored by shedding light on the modalities, scope and dynamics that make them possible and by supporting increased awareness of the local social, moral, traditional, cultural and sustainable aspects of entrepreneurship in facilitating and sustaining the next generation of entrepreneurs. At the academic and policy level, this requires that more research is focused on these key issues. Qatar National Vision 2030 underscores the importance of a process in which academic actors conduct more applied research based on scientific and rigorous criteria and knowledge on how these processes can support entrepreneurship education, as well as other pedagogies and specialized training, and produce teaching materials that can be immediately and practically used.

Finally, it is also important to remember that non-economic variables (such as choices made by individuals) are embedded in economic behaviors (the professional position to which the individual aspires, and for which they want to be trained) and vice versa. This calls for a deconstruction and reconstruction of the relationship between moral values and the role of the community, social institutions, the economy, markets and entrepreneurship. The mechanisms of these interactions need to be studied and understood to enable the development of the necessary instruments required to maximize the chances to develop enterprises aligned to social and cultural needs, as these will have the best chance of succeeding in the longer term. The blockade has provided Qatar with the opportunity as well as the need to do this. If Qatar can succeed in developing such a nuanced and innovative path for its entrepreneurial sector, it will not only secure its future but may also contribute greatly to good entrepreneurial practice on the regional and global level.

Religious Arguments and Counter-Arguments During the Gulf Crisis

SOHAIRA Z. M. SIDDIQUI, GEORGETOWN UNIVERSITY IN QATAR

Perhaps even more shocking than the sudden overnight blockade of Qatar by its closest allies was the timing – the tenth of Ramadan, in the holiest month of the Islamic calendar. Immediately, food trucks were blocked from entering Qatar at its Abu Samra border with Saudi Arabia. This left Qatar's fasting Muslim population concerned over breaking their fast for the last two-thirds of the month and angered over what they saw as a clearly deliberate act by the coalition ranged against them.

Launching the blockade in the middle of the holy month was not the only way in which the Saudi-led coalition introduced religion into the political equation from the outset of the current crisis. In the days that followed, official state clerics and religious institutions in Saudi Arabia began to release statements justifying the blockade in religious terms. Though the use of religion by the anti-Qatar coalition was no more likely to persuade Qatar to concede on key matters of sovereignty, it was intended to legitimize the blockade and appease Saudi religious elites who continue to demand some say in the kingdom's politics.

This use of religious rhetoric as a political instrument was replicated by religious institutions and leaders outside of Saudi Arabia who characterized Qatar's past political actions as challenges to Islam itself. This chapter will first explore the ways in which religion has been used in the realm of policy during the crisis. It will then survey some of the religious justifications of, and responses to, the blockade. Finally, it will analyze what the justifications and responses reveal about the various ways religion interacts with the state across the Arab world in general, and the Gulf Cooperation Council (GCC) countries in particular.

Religion, Legitimacy and the State

Religion has long been recognized as an effective legitimizer of leaders and the specific state policies that they introduce. Historically, one can identify numerous cases in which religion has been used to foster public support, quell unrest, ensure stability, and demonize political opponents. Though modern governments primarily justify their rule through positive policy outcomes, prior to the Enlightenment religion was the sole basis of legitimacy in Europe, where the right to rule was divinely bestowed on a monarch directly from God, and mediated through the church.

The notion of the divine right to rule did not exist in the Islamic model of the caliphate; instead the main duty of the caliph was to safeguard the sanctity of the Muslim community. With the shift from empire to modern nation states in the 20th century, religion ceased to be the main source of legitimacy for rulers, though it continued to serve as an important instrument of legitimacy and power for political elites.

Initially, religion was not a stand-alone area of inquiry in the study of International Relations; yet a focus on instrumentalist theory has enabled religion to emerge as an important factor in assessing the interactions between states in the international system. Instrumentalist theory argues that certain factors such as nationalism and ethnicity are increasingly relevant in the realm of politics and policy as they are highly effective tools to ensure certain political ends.[1] Building on the foundational view that nationalism and ethnicity are political tools, scholars have argued that religion should also be considered a political tool because normative and constructivist factors including culture, identity and values are increasingly important determinants of foreign policy behavior.[2] Some, like Robert Hefner, even go so far as to argue that the use of religion as a political tool is one of the defining features of modern "global politics."[3] Hefner posits that this trend evolved as a response to an attempt at political homogenization through democratization,

---

1   Jonathan Fox and Shmuel Sandler, *Bringing Religion into International Relations*, New York: Palgrave MacMillan, 2006, p. 48.

2   Ibid., p. 45.

3   Robert Hefner, *Civil Islam*, New Jersey: Princeton University Press, 2000, pp. 3–4.

which resulted in widespread ethno-religious revivalism on the international stage.[1]

The uses of religion in politics are multifaceted. While some political elites may use religion for the specific purpose of consolidating the legitimacy of their rule, increasingly it has been used as a tool to justify political policies. When religion is employed in this way, in relatively religiously homogeneous states wherein state legitimacy is also connected to religion, disagreeing with the policy of the state becomes tantamount to resisting religious doctrine. Though religion as a political tool in these circumstances has traditionally been used to consolidate power and shape domestic policy, more recently it has also been used to justify foreign policy actions. The Saudi-led blockade of Qatar, and the religious rhetoric used in justifying it, exemplifies this growing trend.

Religious Justifications and Responses

The original religious defense for the coalition's blockade came from Saudi Arabia's Grand Mufti, Sheikh Abdul Aziz bin Abdullah al-Sheikh. In his *fatwa* (religious judgment), he argued that Saudi Arabia was an Islamic country and actions against Qatar were undertaken for the public welfare (*mas lah a*) of all Muslims, not only Qataris. This justification raises two important points. First, the grand mufti framed the blockade in terms of public welfare, using the term *mas lah a*, an Islamic legal term, with a very specific connotation. *Mas lah a*, broadly speaking, was understood in the Islamic legal tradition as the overarching purpose of the divine law, Sharīʿa. A concept whose genesis stretches back to the 11th century, it was argued by jurists that the purpose of the laws of the Sharīʿa was to ensure the benefit and welfare of its adherents.

Politically, it was understood that the ruler of Muslims had an obligation to ensure the welfare of individuals, and could also create laws and justify

1   Jose Casanova has referred to religions' participating in the public and political spheres as "public religions" and notes their rise since the 1970s. See Jose Casanova, *Public Religions in the Modern World*, Chicago: University of Chicago Press, 1994. For the increasing presence of Islam and Islamic law in the political sphere of Muslim majority countries see Robert Hefner (ed.), *Shari'a Politics: Islamic Law and Society in the Modern World*, Indiana: Indiana University Press, 2011.

them on the basis of public welfare.[1] Thus by justifying the blockade on public welfare grounds, and by referring to Saudi Arabia as an Islamic country, the grand mufti is implicitly arguing that the government of Saudi Arabia is at the helm of the Muslim world and is able to deduce what is in the best interest of *all Muslims*, not just Muslims in Saudi Arabia. In line with this assertion, the mufti pointed out that the Prophet Muhammad was born and received revelation in Mecca, and that Saudi Arabia continues to be the guardian of the two holiest cities in Islam – Mecca and Medina.

Other prominent institutions and individuals within coalition countries also invoked religion to justify their unprecedented political action. Perhaps most famously, the former Grand Mufti of Egypt, Ali Gomaa, traced the roots of the modern Qatari royal family back to an early group of Muslim political dissenters known as the Khawarij. The Khawarij are famous for rebelling against the fourth caliph after the death of the Prophet Muhammad, Ali ibn Abi Talib, and for espousing political and theological views that were eventually held to be heretical.[2]

Ali Gomaa argued that the Khawarij were confronted and defeated, and their descendants in Qatar would suffer the same fate within two years. The timeframe given by Ali Gomaa for the demise of the Qatari royal family and the reference to an earlier heretical group were viewed by many to be illogical on both historical and theological grounds. That aside, similar to the *fatwa* released by the Saudi grand mufti, it does illuminate the ways in which Islam, and Islamic history, have been invoked in support of the blockade. The argument that the Qatari royal family, like the Kharijites before them, are heretical serves a larger purpose than simply legitimizing the blockade; it also justifies fighting them in order to preserve the sanctity of the Muslim community (i.e. the public welfare).[3]

It is no surprise, given the initiation of the blockade by the most senior

---

1   For an overview of duties of the caliph in relation to the Muslim community and the challenges it poses for modern day understandings of Islamic states and legislation see Asifa Quraishi-Landes, 'The Sharia problem with Sharia legislation,' *Ohio North University Law Review*, Vol. 41 (2015), pp. 545–66.

2   For more on the Khawarij and early political debates after the death of the Prophet see W. Montgomery Watt, *The Formative Period of Islamic Thought*, New York: OneWorld Publications, 1998.

3   'Egypt's former grand mufti predicts "extermination" of Qatar,' *Middle East Eye*, 29 June 2017.

political echelon in the coalition countries, that current or former government officials (the grand mufti of Saudi Arabia and the former grand mufti of Egypt respectively), were ready to provide their religious backing. Official religious institutions such as the Supreme Council of the Senior Scholars in both Egypt and Saudi Arabia did the same.

What is more surprising is the decision of non-official, seemingly independent institutions in member states of the anti-Qatar coalition to release statements in support of the blockade. As has been pointed out, the promptness with which these statements were released, and the fact that they were often reported by state media *before* being officially placed on the organizations' websites, indicates that these institutions, by virtue of financial and other ties to the state, were predisposed toward supporting the blockade and the policies of the government.[1]

One such example is the UAE-based Forum for Promoting Peace in Muslim Societies (FPPMS), set up by the Mauritanian scholar Abdullah bin Bayyah in 2014 as a religious body dedicated to furthering peace in the region, especially in light of escalating religious violence. Less than 48 hours after the blockade began, the FPPMS released a statement in support of the move, charging Qatar with inciting political instability, supporting terrorist groups and stoking sectarian conflict.

Though the language of the statement did not invoke public welfare (*mas lah a*) as explicitly as the other justifications did, the general tenor of the statement indicated that the blockade was meant to restore order and stability to the region in response to the detrimental political positions adopted by Qatari decision-makers. The statement concluded with the words of the second Caliph of the Prophet, Umar al-Khattab: "Returning to the truth is better than continuing in falsehood." The use of this statement by Umar – a man recognized by the Muslim community as one of the most righteous and politically astute caliphs – served to emphasize just how egregious the actions of the Qatari government were.

There were several religious responses emanating from inside Qatar. Two, however, are of particular importance. The first was by a senior Qatari Islamic scholar, Sheikh Anwar El-Badawi, who responded directly to the *fatwa* of the grand mufti of Saudi Arabia. He began his response by asking

---

1   Usaama al-Azami, 'Gulf crisis: how autocrats use religious scholars against Qatar,' *Middle East Eye*, 4 August 2017.

the grand mufti to provide scriptural proof in either the Qur'an or the sayings of the Prophet Muhammad (*hadith*), that would support the actions taken by the blockading countries. Invoking the notion of brotherhood and community, El-Badawi argued that verses in the Qur'an explicitly state that one should maintain ties of kinship and brotherhood, and thus the blockade contravened the basic dictates of the religion.[1]

In addition to this response, which gained significant attention, the Doha International Center for Interfaith Dialogue (DICID) organized a seminar titled "The Role of Dialogue in Crisis Solving: Siege of Qatar as an Example." In the seminar, which took place in September 2017, prominent religious scholars such as Dr. Ali Mohiuddin al-Qaradaghi, secretary general of the International Union of Muslim Scholars (IUMS), Dr. Aisha al-Mannai, director of the Mohammad bin Hamad Al Thani Center for Islamic Civilization, and Dr. Ibrahim al-Naimi, chairman of DICID, participated in a discussion with prominent Qatar business leaders.[2] During this exchange, the Islamic scholars present noted that there was no legitimate justification for the blockade, and that Qatar was still willing to engage in dialogue, in line with its commitment to harmonious relations and the legacy of the Prophet.

On a very basic level the various invocations of religion demonstrate the ways in which religion can be employed by the state when constructing foreign policy. Moreover, the systematic defense of the blockade in religious terms also reveals a battle for the hearts and minds of the region's majority Muslim population. By essentially ignoring the appeals of Qatari scholars for discussion and a return to unity, antagonistic scholars in blockading countries were delegitimizing their opinions in order to reduce support for Qatar in Muslim communities. This attempted marginalization strategy can be seen clearly in the treatment of the Qatari-based scholar, Dr. Yusuf al Qaradawi, whose specific case clearly highlights the intersection of state policy and religious de-legitimation of dissident voices.

---

1 'Qatari cleric issues stern religious reminder to Saudi's Grand Mufti over boycott edict,' *5Pillars*, 27 June 2017, https://5pillarsuk.com/2017/06/27/grand-mufti-of-qatars-stern-religious-reminder-to-grand-mufti-of-saudi-over-boycott-edict/.

2 Irfan Bukhari, 'Blockade unethical and un-Islamic: Seminar,' *The Peninsula Qatar*, 29 September 2017.

State Contempt and Scholarly Justification: The Case of Qaradawi

The previously mentioned International Union of Muslim Scholars (IUMS), and its founder Sheikh Yusuf al Qaradawi, are important actors in facilitating our understanding of the realpolitik and religious tensions that existed between Qatar and the blockading countries, which culminated in the 2017 crisis. Set up in 2004 in Doha and supported by the then Amir, Hamad bin Khalifa, the IUMS purports to be an independent, non-governmental association of 90,000 Muslim scholars across the globe that provides representation for Muslims and offers Islamic scholarly responses to local and international issues. Interestingly, its vice president between 2004 and 2013 was Sheikh Abdullah bin Bayyah, the founder of the FPPMS, a long-time defender of Qatar before altering his position when the blockade commenced.

Qaradawi studied in Al Azhar, receiving his doctorate in 1973, and was part of the Muslim Brotherhood during Gamal Abdel Nasser's reign in Egypt. When President Nasser launched his campaign against the Brotherhood, Qaradawi fled to Qatar in 1961 where in subsequent decades he established himself as an important and charismatic Islamic thinker. However, Qaradawi's influence was not limited to Qatar alone. In 1994, Saudi Arabia honored him with the prestigious King Faisal International Prize, and in Dubai he was given an international award as the "Islamic Personality of the Year" in 2000. At the same time, Qaradawi was considered an informal spiritual and intellectual leader for the Muslim Brotherhood. Though he had no official position in the Brotherhood itself, this role would eventually set him at odds with other Gulf states. Qaradawi's popularity was in large part fueled by his show on the Al Jazeera news network, *Shariah and Life*. This provided him with the stage to convey on a weekly basis his legal opinions and views to a large audience across the Arab and Muslim world. By the time of the Arab Spring in 2011, Qaradawi had developed an international reputation as a firebrand who supported many organizations and causes opposed by other Gulf states, including the Brotherhood and Hamas in Gaza. [1] His profile was further extended when

---

1   Sudarsan Raghavan and Joby Warrick, 'How a 91-year-old imam came to symbolize the feud between Qatar and its neighbors,' *Washington Post*, 27 June 2017.

he backed the revolutions in Libya and Egypt, in noticeable contrast to the more subdued position of the then grand mufti of Egypt, Ali Gomaa.

In 2013, when Abdel Fattah Al Sisi overturned the short-lived Muslim Brotherhood government of Mohamed Morsi in Egypt, the organization became enemy number one not only in Egypt but across the Arab Gulf, with the exception of Qatar. In the same year, Ali Gomaa engaged in a rancorous debate with Qaradawi on the legitimacy of the military coup that ousted Morsi. Gomaa argued that Morsi's supporters were *Khawarij*, a term that Qaradawi had himself used in his condemnation of the Egyptian army's forceful attack on those protesting in favor of the Brotherhood. At the conclusion of this exchange, Gomaa accused Qaradawi of being senile.[1]

In this climate, Bin Bayyah resigned from his post in IUMS as Qaradawi found himself increasingly isolated among high-level Muslim scholars. What is noteworthy is the response of Qatar to this situation. In November 2013, Qatar and its GCC partners, who supported the new Sisi government, had signed the Riyadh Agreement. It demanded that Qatar extradite Brotherhood sympathizers, which most assumed implicitly meant Qaradawi. This did not happen, though his television show, *Shariah and Life*, was taken off the air without much fanfare.[2]

Four years later, in June 2017, a few days after the embargo of Qatar began, Saudi Arabia, Bahrain, the UAE and Egypt placed Qaradawi on a terrorist list, his views now unacceptable to scholars in coalition member states who followed the policy positions of their governments.[3] Subsequently, IUMS was placed on the same list.[4] The grand mufti of Saudi Arabia even linked the Brotherhood with the Islamic State of Iraq and the Levant (ISIS) and Jabhat al Nusrat, on religious grounds,[5] thus effectively delegitimizing the Brotherhood by implying that it was outside the Islamic polity.

1   David H. Warren, 'The *Ulam* and the Arab uprisings 2011-13: considering Yusuf al-Qaradawi, the "Global Mufti," between the Muslim Brotherhood, the Islamic legal tradition, and Qatari foreign policy,' *New Middle Eastern Studies*, No. 4, 2014.

2   David H. Warren, 'Qatari support for the Muslim Brotherhood is more than just realpolitik, it has a long, personal history,' *Maydan*, 12 July 2017.

3   '59 people, 12 groups with Qatar links on "terror list",' *Al Jazeera*, 9 June 2017.

4   'Arab states blacklist Islamist groups, individuals in Qatar boycott,' *Reuters*, 22 November 2017.

5   'Activists circulate Saudi ruling that the Muslim Brotherhood is among "righteous Islamic groups",' *Middle East Monitor*, 19 June 2017.

Conclusion and Lessons Learned

The call by Qatari scholars for Muslim unity in response to the blockade has not influenced the views of political or religious leaders in coalition countries. Ironically, Ali Gomaa and Sheikh Abdul Aziz bin Abdullah have justified the blockade by locating Qatar outside the unified Muslim community, and implying that it can only reenter after it agrees to coalition demands, which include breaking with the Muslim Brotherhood. In this sense, the animus against the Brotherhood is state policy for coalition members and many senior scholars within these countries. As a result, leading scholars have attempted to link the country as a political entity to the views of the Brotherhood, thereby blurring the lines between religious pluralism and state policy.

The Domestic Policy Opportunities
of an International Blockade

JOCELYN SAGE MITCHELL, NORTHWESTERN UNIVERSITY IN QATAR

Since the beginning of the diplomatic crisis in June 2017, Qatar has been busy addressing numerous large-scale geopolitical, economic and security challenges. Yet the small kingdom has gone beyond these pressing issues to engage in extensive domestic policy shifts. These policies range from expanded citizenship rights to stronger labor protections to increased foreign business and investment opportunities. This presents us with a puzzle: with all of the international demands on Qatari political and financial resources, why is domestic policy such a priority?

In this chapter I suggest that Qatar's rulers are seizing the opportunities provided by this period of uncertainty to make surprisingly strong progress on societal issues that have been simmering for far longer than the blockade itself. The system-wide shock of the blockade has created a rapidly changing situation in the Gulf Cooperation Council (GCC), in which the normal parameters of social, economic and institutional rules are in flux and the rules of the political game can be redefined.[1] These moves are an indication that Qatar's leaders are using the crisis to their advantage, by pushing through domestic policy goals that may not only reshape their own country but the GCC as a whole.

---

1   The author thanks Nick Mitchell, Scott Curtis, Rory Miller and Zahra Babar for useful comments, and Paul Musgrave for astute advice on an earlier version of this work. Hind Alansari (ethnographic interviews) and Sherin Karawia (Twitter analysis) provided excellent research assistance.
Guillermo O'Donnell and Philippe C. Schmitter, *Transitions from Authoritarian Rule: Tentative Conclusions about Uncertain Democracies*, Baltimore: Johns Hopkins University Press, 1986.

The GCC Split: From Conservative Unity to Independent Competition

The GCC was formed in 1981 by the six monarchies of the Arabian Peninsula – Bahrain, Kuwait, Oman, Qatar, Saudi Arabia, and the UAE – to protect against Iraqi and Iranian encroachment. Iraq's invasion and occupation of oil-rich Kuwait in 1990 demonstrated the limitations of the GCC as a security actor. Yet the GCC has fared much better at protecting its autocratic rulers against *internal* threats. Under Saudi Arabia's dominating influence, the GCC has followed a conservative path, acting (or failing to act) as a unified bloc on sensitive social and political issues to provide a measure of political cover from citizen dissent.[1] This is not to say that the GCC member states have always been in lockstep; jockeying over national luxury airlines or ownership of the GCC's tallest spire are examples of competitive spirit. But when it has come to upending long-standing socio-economic structures such as citizenship and labor policies, all six countries have relied on the united front to move forward slowly or not at all.

The GCC bloc is united no more. Following the launch of the June 2017 blockade, coordination among GCC members on economic, social and political matters unraveled. In its place, Qatar has pursued a raft of progressive policy changes, which promote the country's individual interests over the conservative preferences of the GCC as a whole.

Consider the laws of citizenship. Before the blockade, like all members of the GCC, Qatar had exclusive and patriarchal citizenship laws, which passed down citizenship only from father to child (Law No. 38 of 2005). Being born in Qatar gives no claim to citizenship: even children of Qatari women married to non-Qatari men do not receive citizenship upon birth. Nor do long-term expatriate residents, some of whom have lived and worked in the country for generations. Then, in August 2017, two months after the start of the blockade, Qatar became the first GCC member state to move toward bestowing non-citizens with economic benefits similar to those of full citizens – including free education, free health care and preferential hiring – as well as the stability of permanent residency rather than temporary visas that must be renewed regularly.

---

1   Sean Foley, *The Arab Gulf States: Beyond Oil and Islam*, Boulder: Lynne Rienner, 2010.

Labor policies toward migrant workers have also seen significant disruption post-blockade. Historically, the Gulf states, located along the trade routes of the Gulf and the Indian Ocean, have been host to significant migrant worker populations. Yet it was the oil booms of the 20th century that led to the exponential increase in populations, to the point where expatriates represented 70% of the region's workforce by 2012.[1] Qatar, along with the UAE, has one of the GCC's highest ratios of migrant labor to citizen population – with foreign workers outnumbering Qatari citizens by a ratio of roughly 10 to one. The massive influx of foreign labor has resulted in much international scrutiny over worker rights and conditions.

These concerns have intensified greatly since Qatar won its 2010 bid to host the 2022 FIFA World Cup, the world's biggest sporting competition. Organizations such as Human Rights Watch and the International Labour Organization (ILO) have drawn attention to tragic cases and called for major reform. Here, too, post-blockade, we have seen rapid change that moves Qatar to the front of the GCC pack – alongside or even ahead of Kuwait's 2015 labor reforms. Qatar has established a dispute committee to handle workers' concerns (Law No. 13 of 2017), increased legal protections for domestic workers (Law No. 15 of 2017) and set a minimum wage. These moves are not cosmetic and have been accompanied by the promise of additional changes in the future. "If half of what is promised is actually done," one insider to the labor rights reform process explained to me in February 2018, "the country will be reshaped in three years." In recognition of these new measures and future plans, the ILO dropped its complaint against Qatar in October 2017.[2]

The GCC in recent years had slowly been working toward increased economic integration. These agreements included a customs union (in 2003) and a common market (in 2008).[3] Since 2008, intra-GCC trade has

---

1   Omar AlShehabi, 'Histories of Migration to the Gulf,' in Abdulhadi Khalaf, Omar AlShehabi, and Adam Hanieh (eds.), *Transit States: Labour, Migration & Citizenship in the Gulf*, London: Pluto Press, 2015, pp. 3–38.

2   'Complaint concerning non-observance by Qatar of the Forced Labour Convention,' 331st Session of the International Labour Office (ILO) Governing Body, Geneva, http://www.ilo.org/wcmsp5/groups/public/---ed_norm/---relconf/documents/meetingdocument/wcms_586479.pdf

3   Karen E. Young, 'Self-Imposed Barriers to Economic Integration in the GCC,' Washington, D.C., *Arab Gulf States Institute in Washington*, 4 August 2017, http://www.agsiw.org/self-imposed-barriers-economic-integration-gcc/

increased substantially, and in 2014 member states signed up to a GCC-wide value-added tax (VAT) on goods and services, set to unroll in 2018. The VAT was intended to help certain member states deal with budget deficits and unsustainable energy subsidies.[1] While Saudi Arabia and the UAE implemented their 5% VAT in January 2018 and Bahrain is expected to launch the tax by mid-2018, Kuwait, Oman and Qatar have not yet followed through on their previous agreements. It appears that Qatar is happy to shoulder this economic burden to avoid the domestic dissatisfaction now being expressed by Saudi and Emirati citizens over additional fees on everyday items.[2]

The post-blockade economic competition between the GCC states extends to relations with the expatriate business community and foreign investors. In Qatar, the promised "sin tax" on alcohol in July 2017 never occurred – a clear sign that the country's leadership is less interested in generating extra revenues than in keeping the expatriate community content. Along with the expansion of programs providing free visas, visas-on-arrival, and visa extensions (Law No. 14 of 2017), Qatar is changing the rules of foreign investment and ownership to allow non-Qataris to own real estate and to fully own their businesses in-country without the need to partner with Qatari citizens. All of these moves place Qatar in direct competition with its GCC neighbors over business and investment opportunities.

The Domestic Political Calculus

The uncertainty engendered by the current crisis has allowed for substantive movement on issues that were previously blocked by external and domestic forces that favored the status quo conservatism. The groundswell of nationalism in response to the blockade is providing the fuel for the state's forward momentum. Some of the policy shifts have been broadly popular among the population for a long time – such as the expansion of residency rights to children of Qatari mothers. But until the crisis, their

---

1   Jim Krane, 'Stability versus Sustainability: Energy Policy in the Gulf Monarchies,' *Cambridge Working Papers in Economics*, Cambridge: University of Cambridge, February 2013. https://www.repository.cam.ac.uk/bitstream/handle/1810/246270/cwpe1304.pdf?sequence=1&isAllowed=y

2   Simeon Kerr and Ahmed Al Omran, 'Saudi Arabia and UAE introduce 5% VAT in bid to narrow deficits,' *Financial Times*, 2 January 2018.

implementation had been hindered by a powerful minority opposed to such changes. Other policies, however, were unpopular – even destabilizing – such as increased rights for migrant labor and foreign business interests. In both of these areas, decision-makers are nevertheless seizing the opportunity to move forward.

Powerful bursts of nationalism may provide opportunities for change in any country, and Qatar is taking full advantage of this moment. The artistic images of the amir ("Tamim Al Majid"), which have appeared throughout Doha on cars, buildings, billboards, t-shirts, mugs and even gelato, are visual evidence of a nationalism that has surprised, and even overwhelmed, Qataris and non-Qatari residents alike. On 1 August 2017, a 26-year-old Pakistani expatriate expressed her feelings of pride and solidarity in Qatar as follows:

> I was very proud of the way Qatar responded, with such elegance, with so much dignity, with so much patience. I think that really made everyone who lives here, it made them proud to be a part of this country, whether or not they are from here, it made them proud … I think this blockade now tells you what it means to be a Qatari. I think now is when nationalism is founded. Now you can tell clearly who you are and what being Qatari means to you. And I think it also became more inclusive. Before it was very exclusive. So everybody who lives here, you feel like you are part of the country now.

Likewise, on 17 August 2017, a 27-year-old Qatari mused on his own changing feelings of patriotism and the shifting mindset of the citizens around him:

> Everyone who knows me … I actually criticize our government for certain things that it has been doing. But ever since this whole situation started, I'm actually impressed with our Qatari government … Since this whole thing has started, there have been a lot of individual efforts when it comes to showing the emotions that are within … and something I've noticed is the government is actually looking into this and actually supporting some individuals, and this makes me happy because there is a line of communication between upstairs and downstairs, and this is great, and I'm very optimistic. This whole thing – really, I mean, I have to say this – benefited Qatar so much. We see

private investors or actually individuals investing in and providing resources to the country, when it comes to the food industry, when it comes to the import-export business, whatever. Beforehand, people would rely on government support for everything. Now people are taking things into their own hands and trying to help the government in providing for the citizens, which is great.

To illustrate the ways in which Qatar has used this nationalism to push through its policy priorities, consider the case of the children of Qatari mothers and non-Qatari fathers. In 2013 and 2014, I conducted two original, nationally representative surveys of Qatari citizens' attitudes and opinions.[1] Both times, nine out of 10 Qataris – men and women – supported a change in the laws to allow Qatari women to pass their citizenship on to their children. Qataris have not been silent about these concerns: local media frequently broadcast complaints from those who are excluded from citizenship and its corresponding state-distributed benefits.[2] While the Qatari government acknowledged these concerns and pledged to review the laws in its 2011 National Development Strategy, there had been no discernable progress on this issue in subsequent years.

Why, then, did they change the law in August 2017? It seems that a small but powerful conservative minority in Qatar, coupled with the GCC-wide preference to maintain the status quo, had hindered movement on this issue. The humanitarian crisis caused by the blockade gave the Qatari regime the domestic political cover to act. Thousands of citizens across the GCC are

---

1   Jocelyn Sage Mitchell, Christina M. Paschyn, Sadia Mir, Kirsten Pike, and Tanya Kane, 'In *majaalis al-hareem:* The complex professional and personal choices of Qatari women,' *DIFI Family Research and Proceedings*, Vol. 4, 2015. The 2017 survey (n=798) was made possible by a grant (UREP 12-016-5-007) from the Qatar National Research Fund (QNRF) and a supplementary grant from Georgetown University in Qatar. The 2014 survey (n=1,049) was made possible by a grant (UREP 15-035-5-013) from the QNRF. The statements made herein are solely the responsibility of the author.

2   Amal Mohammed Al-Malki, 'Public Policy and Identity,' in M. Evren Tok, Lolwah Alkhater, and Leslie A. Pal (eds.), *Policy Making in a Transformative State: The Case of Qatar*, London: Palgrave Macmillan, 2016, pp. 260–261. See the Twitter handle and hashtag ImHalfQatari for many of these complaints, which concern educational scholarships, employment opportunities, land ownership, and even the ability to marry and have children of their own.

intermarried. But with spousal transfer of citizenship difficult at best, most retain their home country's citizenship even when marrying, living and working in another GCC state. When the blockading countries recalled their citizens from Qatar and forced Qatari citizens to leave their countries, families found themselves split apart during the holy month of Ramadan. Qatar's granting of permanent residency to previously excluded members of society is a shrewd political move to use the immediate humanitarian crisis of the blockade to solve a longer-term domestic problem. And public approval on Twitter was immediate, with many encouraging further expansion of the law to give spouses and children of Qatari women full citizenship.[1] As of February 2018, the draft of this law is under discussion in the Internal and Foreign Affairs Committee of the Shura Council (the national advisory council).

This permanent residency law will also extend benefits to certain long-term expatriates who have offered valuable contributions to Qatari society and the local economy, and may be the first step toward full citizenship for these expatriates as well. According to the Permanent Population Committee's 2017 five-year population policy, granting citizenship to these expatriates is in line with objectives set out in the Qatar National Vision 2030: It increases the number of citizens, and it promotes social stability and the integration of these expatriates into the existing citizenry.[2] The amir has explicitly praised Qatari residents alongside citizens, including in his speech to the UN General Assembly in September 2017, when he stated, "Allow me, on this occasion and from this podium, to express my pride in my Qatari people, along with the multinational and multicultural residents in Qatar."[3] Versions of this quote have reappeared in many public venues in Qatar since then, including at the leBlockade exhibit at Katara Cultural

---

1   The hashtag Permanent Residency Card (in Arabic; http://bit.ly/2Bfdy53) was used to express support (e.g., http://bit.ly/2nLadDg), and to advocate for other groups to receive permanent residency (http://bit.ly/2GVi6Oh) and even full citizenship (http://bit.ly/2BgMMJy)

2   Permanent Population Committee, 'The Population Policy of the State of Qatar 2017–2022,' https://www.mdps.gov.qa/en/statistics/Statistical%20Releases/Population/Population/2017/population_policy_2017_EN.pdf

3   Amir Sheikh Tamim bin Hamad Al Thani, 'Speech to the United Nations General Assembly,' *The Peninsula Qatar*, 19 September 2017, https://www.thepeninsulaqatar.com/article/19/09/2017/In-Full-Text-The-speech-of-Qatar-Emir-at-the-opening-session-of-UN-General-Assembly

Village in November–December 2017. Expatriates have taken note. On 12 August 2017, a 24-year-old Qatari of Egyptian background explained, "My patriotism has been affected. I used to be a very non-patriotic person to any country and now, obviously, I do feel that this crisis has brought people together, and for the first time, I feel that now we in Qatar are a community, and even the expats, we all care and we consider it here our home."

On the other hand, the domestic policy moves related to labor reforms and foreign business interests challenge, and even collide, with deeply ingrained public preferences. Here, too, we see how Qatar has used nationalist sentiment to push through important, albeit unpopular, domestic policies. In general, Qataris have both sociocultural and economic reasons for supporting the existing economic status quo that gives advantage to nationals over expatriates and retains worker control in the hands of citizens.[1] These economic structures have been an integral part of citizen economic wellbeing, as well as the regime's political and social stability, for decades. Again, the forward movement on this issue clearly highlights Qatar's strategy of using the current crisis to implement measures that are politically *necessary* (improving labor conditions and diversifying the investment environment) but are not politically *popular*.

To help facilitate the creation and implementation of these new laws and regulations, the amir altered the membership of the Shura Council, with several families losing their appointments and new families ushered in, including, for the first time, four women (Amiri Decree No. 22 of 2017). This was done for a political purpose: to stack the Shura Council with like-minded progressives who are ready to move forward on contentious domestic issues. This is not to say that the changes will be easy or quick; Qatar's executive and bureaucratic capacities are far less transformative and autonomous than rentier theorists assume.[2] But the political will for

---

1   Zahra R. Babar, 'Population, Power, and Distributional Politics in Qatar,' *Journal of Arabian Studies*, Vol. 5, No. 2 (2015), pp. 138–155; Abdoulaye Diop, Kien Trung Le, Trevor Johnston, and Michael Ewers, 'Citizen's Attitudes Towards Migrant Workers in Qatar,' *Migration and Development*, Vol. 6, No. 1 (2017), pp. 144–160.

2   Jocelyn Sage Mitchell and Leslie A. Pal, 'Policy Making in Qatar: The Macro-Policy Framework,' in Tok, Alkhater and Pal, *Policy Making in a Transformative State*, pp. 65–96; Kristian Coates Ulrichsen, *Qatar and the Arab Spring*, London: Hurst, 2014, pp. 80–94. For a parallel viewpoint on Saudi Arabia, see Steffen Hertog, *Princes, Brokers, and Bureaucrats: Oil and the State in Saudi Arabia*, Ithaca: Cornell University Press, 2010.

change is there, and it is gaining momentum.

Conclusion and Lessons Learned

Inside Qatar, these major domestic policy moves may herald more change to come, particularly in the area of political reforms. It is of consequence that one of the first responses to the diplomatic crisis was a "GCC Unity Blog" on WordPress.com, signed by more than 700 GCC academics and intellectuals, which called for increased citizen involvement in political affairs.

This sort of politicization has been evident previously in response to grave external threats to sovereignty. Kuwait pursued a similar strategy in both the 1960s and 1990s to gain political legitimacy in the face of Iraqi territorial threats.[1] In a move that challenged the theoretical assumption that oil wealth enables rulers to prevent the formation of semi-autonomous parliaments, the exogenous threat to Kuwait spurred the creation and, later, the re-institution of the Kuwaiti National Assembly, which today wields significant power in the kingdom's affairs.

Likewise, we may see increased democratization in Qatar as it seeks to differentiate itself from the blockading countries. An obvious political reform would be the long-awaited elections to the Shura Council. In his November 2017 speech to the Shura Council, the amir noted that "the government is currently preparing for the Advisory Council elections," which are scheduled to take place in 2019.[2] Qatari citizens themselves expect these elections to occur: my 2013 survey showed that an overwhelming majority of Qataris (90%) favored elections to their national legislature, as promised by their 2004 constitution.[3] "If there ever was censorship revolving around political topics, at this time there is none," a 24-year-old Qatari citizen explained to me in early July 2017, before continuing,

---

1   Michael Herb, *The Wages of Oil: Parliaments and Economic Development in Kuwait and the UAE*. Ithaca: Cornell University Press, 2014.

2   Amir Sheikh Tamim bin Hamad Al Thani, 'Speech to the Shura Council,' 14 November 2017, *The Peninsula Qatar*, https://thepeninsulaqatar.com/article/14/11/2017/Full-text-of-Emir%E2%80%99s-speech-at-the-Advisory-Council

3   Jocelyn Sage Mitchell, *Beyond Allocation: The Politics of Legitimacy in Qatar*, Unpublished PhD Dissertation, Georgetown University, Washington, D.C., 2013.

"Political conversations are occurring in the majlis [private gatherings] and in public too."

While my survey research demonstrates that the majority of Qataris have a low self-assessment of their political efficacy,[1] this moment may increase their desire for greater political voice. As one 55-year-old Qatari citizen stated on 17 August 2017,

> This tragedy has proven that the people are completely absent from the decision-making scene ... I wish that Qatar returns to its people and takes them into consideration to initiate a parliament or a legitimate authority that allows people to participate in the political scene ... We want true changes that allow more inclusivity for the people.

Qatari advances on the domestic policy front may come to be the defining outcome of this diplomatic crisis, especially if the blockade continues over the longer term. The blockade is now widely seen as a "strategic failure" in terms of achieving its original foreign policy goals.[2] But its domestic repercussions continue to reverberate throughout the GCC. Across the now-closed border, Saudi Arabia is also undertaking surprising moves of its own, such as allowing women to drive and recopening movie theaters. These shifts have led one international commentator, Thomas Friedman, to opine that Saudi Arabia is experiencing its own, albeit top-down, Arab Spring.[3] Likewise in the UAE, in October 2017, Emirati women married to non-Emirati men received the right to apply for citizenship for their children after they turn six years old (Federal Decree Law No. 16 of 2017).

Tumult in the Gulf has a way of provoking unintended change. In the 1990s, the Iraqi invasion and occupation of Kuwait resulted in a national identity, political system and media sector that are very different from those that exist across the rest of the GCC. Now, the blockade that was meant to

---

1   Justin J. Gengler and Jocelyn Sage Mitchell, 'A Hard Test of Individual Heterogeneity in Response Scale Usage: Evidence from Qatar,' *International Journal of Public Opinion Research* Vol. 30, Issue 1 (2018), pp.102-124

2   Gabriel Collins, *Anti-Qatar Embargo Grinds Toward Strategic Failure*, Baker Institute for Public Policy, Rice University, https://www.bakerinstitute.org/media/files/files/7299ac91/bi-brief-012218-ces-qatarembargo.pdf

3   Thomas Friedman, 'Saudi Arabia's Arab Spring, at last,' *The New York Times*, 23 November 2017.

reinforce the conservative status quo is instead leading to rapid change across the GCC. Qatar's next moves will further illuminate the unintended consequences of a miscalculated blockade.

Qatar Foundation: A Civil Society Actor Responds to a Crisis

MARYAH B. AL-DAFA, HAMAD BIN KHALIFA UNIVERSITY

In 1995, Sheikh Hamad bin Khalifa Al Thani assumed the leadership of Qatar. From the outset of his rule, he demonstrated a clear intention to change the country significantly and to put Qatar on the international map. At the heart of these plans, and one of his earliest policy initiatives, was the decision to establish the Qatar Foundation (QF) in 1995. This was the first non-governmental organization in Qatar and its launch was part of an overall vision inspired by the limitless ambition of a new national leadership, which would be seen time and again over the next two decades.

Sheikha Moza, wife of the then amir, is the co-founder of Qatar Foundation and currently serves as its chairperson. When the Foundation was established, it was staffed by only a few people, all of whom shared the QF leadership's commitment to contribute to the development of Qatar, its aspiration to change the quality of life in the country, and its belief in the power of knowledge to drive forward societal advancement. As the vision statement on the Foundation's website explains to this day: "Through education and research, Qatar Foundation leads human, social, and economic development of Qatar; making Qatar a nation that can be a vanguard for productive change in the region and a role model for the broader international community."[1]

From its earliest days, and up to the present time, the Foundation's vision has been grounded in a belief in the importance of creating a wide range of educational and research opportunities in line with the highest international

---

1　For the vision and mission of the Qatar Foundation see https://www.qf.org.qa/about/about

standards.[1] This journey started with the development of a model for K-12 schools,[2] with the first school opening its doors to its inaugural, and smallest, class of students soon after the establishment of QF. In subsequent years, QF embarked on an equally ambitious program of attracting some of the world's best higher-education institutes to Doha. In time, one British and six American universities, one French business school, and a home-grown research university named after the amir who founded QF (Hamad Bin Khalifa University), all opened their doors in Education City, the appropriately named sprawling knowledge ecosystem built under the auspices of QF in the Doha suburbs.[3]

The Foundation, and the Education City where it is based, were created as a hub for knowledge and innovation and as a crucial catalyst for greater choice in education and health and for social progress in Qatar. Beyond its academic and research institutes, the Foundation also plays an essential role in creating centers that add value to Qatar's development in culture, literacy and policy. The launch of the blockade against Qatar in June 2017 tested this wide-ranging and important mandate in unprecedented and previously unimagined ways.

The Foundation Responds to a Regional Crisis

Tensions between Qatar and Saudi Arabia can be traced back to the establishment of Saudi Arabia in the early 1930s, when the kingdom's founder, Abdulaziz ibn Saud, attempted to claim large parts of Qatar for his kingdom. Since then, and especially after Qatar became an independent state in 1971, it has repeatedly been forced to defend its sovereignty and territorial

---

1   Arwa Ibnouf, Jane Knight and Lois Dou, 'The Evolution of Qatar as an Education Hub: Moving to a knowledge-based economy,' in Jane Knight (ed.), *International Education Hubs: Student, Talent, Knowledge Innovation Model*, Dordrecht: Springer Science, 2014.

2   This term is used in education in the United States and some other countries to describe school grade system prior to third-level. These grades are kindergarten (K) and the 1st through the 12th grade (1-12).

3   The six American universities are Cornell University (2001), Texas A&M University (2003), Carnegie Mellon University (2004), Georgetown University (2005), Northwestern University (2008); the French business school is HEC Paris (2010); the British university is University College London (UCL) (2010).

integrity from Saudi encroachment. On coming to power in 1995, Sheikh Hamad demonstrated a willingness to stand up to his much larger Gulf neighbor to protect the interests of his country and its ambitions. This led to a further worsening in relations, which culminated in the early 2000s with Riyadh withdrawing its ambassador from Doha in protest over the coverage of the Al Jazeera news network.

Despite these prior clashes, no one expected that overnight, and parallel to an orchestrated propaganda frenzy, Saudi Arabia, Bahrain, the United Arab Emirates (UAE) and Egypt would cut off ties with Qatar based on its alleged support for terrorism. This decision to launch a blockade, combined with the extreme hostility expressed toward Qatar in the media and government circles of neighboring states in subsequent weeks and months, presented a shocking new reality for Qatar. At the same time, the Foundation was hit with a new reality of its own – it was now a central civil society actor in Qatar in the face of a blockade and diplomatic boycott that not only targeted Qatar's foreign policy choices but also seemed to undermine its legitimacy as a society and a state.

On top of this, the schools, universities and research centers under the Qatar Foundation umbrella are home to a diverse group of students, faculty and staff from all over the world, including many from the four main blockading nations (Saudi Arabia, Bahrain, the UAE and Egypt), as well as other secondary actors who cut ties (Yemen, Libya, Mauritania, Comoros Islands and the Maldives) or chose to downgrade relations with Qatar (Jordan, Djibouti, Chad and Niger). Some of these students, staff and faculty members, who had not already departed for home at the end of the academic year, now found themselves ordered back by their governments. The Middle East has experienced much upheaval over the decades but this demand that citizens leave their jobs, educations and lives as part of a political clash with their host countries was unprecedented. Some blockading countries, notably the UAE and Bahrain, even threatened their citizens with legal action if they showed any support for or empathy with Qatar.

This was a traumatic experience with significant practical implications, in particular for those staff and students who had made a life in Qatar over previous years. The first step undertaken by the Foundation to counter this difficult and stressful situation was to provide support for anyone affected by the demand to give up their lives and return home. In formulating and executing a response to this predicament, the Foundation demonstrated in real time a commitment to its mandate to promote the values of social progress and tolerance through education. All nationals from blockading or boycotting countries were reassured that the Foundation valued their presence in Qatar and it was made clear that no student, professor or staff member from the countries in question would be pressured to cut ties or ever be asked to leave. The Foundation cooperated with the academic and research institutions under the Qatar Foundation umbrella in this task. Education City's universities began working with their staff, faculty and researchers to convey the QF message that political differences should not pose an obstacle to education, research or community development.

The crisis also provided opportunities to develop camaraderie and closer interactions among students, faculty and staff in the different academic and research institutions across Education City. In one representative example, QF organized for all staff and students to come together to watch the amir's speech at the United Nations in September 2017. This important statement on Qatar's efforts to adapt to the realities of the blockade focused on the themes of perseverance and pride in Qatar's diversity. "Qatar had refused to yield to pressure," the amir explained, before expressing his country's readiness to resolve differences through compromise and calling for "unconditional dialogue based on mutual respect for sovereignty."[1]

The Foundation was established as a place where critical thinking and debate would not only be encouraged but demanded. In these terms, the QF scholarly and research ecosystem also offered an ideal platform for numerous dynamic discussions exploring the causes and implications of the crisis, as well as the possible opportunities for resolving it in a fair and comprehensive manner. These initiatives were both faculty- and student-driven and often were led by faculty and students cooperating together.

For example, in mid-September 2017, experts from across the region gathered to share their insights on the crisis in an event titled "Crisis in the GCC: Causes, Consequences, and Prospects," before an audience of more than 300 that was hosted by Georgetown University's research institute, the Center for International and Regional Studies (CIRS). In an example of faculty-student cooperation, Georgetown and its Al Liwan Qatari Student Club hosted a lecture by Sheikh Abdullah bin Mohammed bin Saud Al

---

1   See General Debate of the 72 Session of the United Nations General Assembly, 19 September 2017 https://gadebate.un.org/en/72/qatar

Thani, chief executive officer of Qatar Investment Authority (QIA), and a member of the Supreme Council for Economic Affairs and Investment, as part of a series of events to commemorate Qatar National Day. The talk, which was open to the public, was held under the theme of "Ingredients of Qatar's Success Under the Blockade." As part of the same series of events, Abdullah bin Hamad Al Attiyah, formerly Qatar's deputy prime minister, minister of energy and industry, and managing director of Qatar Petroleum, gave a talk titled "The Resiliency of Qatar's Growth: The Economic Blockade is a Blessing in Disguise." In the wake of the first US-Qatari Strategic Dialogue, which took place in January 2018 in Washington, D.C., US State Department veteran Daniel Benjamin visited Georgetown to offer his insights into recent shifts in American policy toward the Gulf region in the context of the blockade. The following March, Georgetown co-hosted alongside the Al Jazeera Center for Studies, a panel discussion on "The New Security Architecture in the Gulf in the Wake of the Crisis," that was broadcast live on Al Jazeera and included contributions from local journalists and intellectuals as well as Georgetown and HBKU scholars.

In October 2017, Northwestern University in Qatar, which is a leading provider of media research, education and scholarship in the Middle East, hosted its own major event – The Media Industries Forum – featuring prominent editors and correspondents analyzing fake news, the impact of social media and the role of global reporting in the Gulf crisis. Under the headline "International Media and the Blockade," a panel of experts, which included senior Qatari journalists and international correspondents from *Time* magazine and BuzzFeed News, looked at the ways in which the crisis had been covered in regional and international media outlets in its first six months. Other Northwestern events addressing the crisis included a keynote speech by Sheikh Saif bin Ahmed Al Thani, director of Qatar's Government Communications Office.

Hamad Bin Khalifa University, a public university founded in 2010 as an emerging research university inside QF, is committed to serving as a "catalyst for transformative change in Qatar and the region while having global impact."[1] Since the outbreak of hostilities in June 2017, it has also been very active in holding lectures, discussions and events on the crisis. These have

---

1   For an overview of HBKU's vision, mandate and programs see https://hbku.edu.
     qa/en/about-hamad-bin-khalifa-university

addressed a wide range of relevant topics including a panel discussion, hosted by the university's College of Islamic Studies, on "Qatar After the Blockade: Impact and Prospects." This high-profile event saw local and international experts assess the political, economic, legal and social aspects of the blockade. HBKU has also offered several public lectures and discussions on the blockade that have examined, among other things, the various legal dimensions of the blockade, and (under the auspices of the Dean's Lecture Series) the effectiveness of economic sanctions as a foreign policy tool in the context of the current crisis. Daniel J. Martin, the president of Seattle Pacific University, also gave a highly topical lecture at HBKU under the patronage of Sheikh Abdullah bin Nasser bin Khalifa Al Thani, Qatar's prime minister and minister of interior, on the evolving role of the education sector in light of the blockade. The College of Humanities and Social Sciences also held a public talk on economic sanctions as a foreign policy tool in the context of the recent blockade.

Besides its role in providing expert analysis on the blockade, HBKU also played two other important functions in the midst of the crisis. At short notice, it worked with the Attorney General's Office, as well as with the compensation and claims committee, to support a national priority: to place Qatari students who were forced to abandon their studies in blockading countries in higher education entities in Qatar. On a more strategic level, HBKU also pro-actively built on existing research cooperation and educational ties with peer institutions in friendly neighboring states. One example of this was a five-year partnership agreement that HBKU signed with the prestigious Kuwait Institute for Scientific Research (KISR), to collaborate on and fund joint research projects.[1] Hamad Bin Khalifa University also signed an agreement with Istanbul Sabahttin Zaim University (IZU). As HBKU President Dr. Ahmad M. Hasnah explained: "We are fully committed to ensuring that future generations of global leaders are better equipped to address key issues facing the Arab and Muslim region, which will have a positive impact on our economy."

---

1   'HBKU & Kuwait institute sign deal to boost research efforts,' *The Peninsula Qatar*, 30 November 2017.

Conclusion and Lessons Learned

Until the establishment of QF, Qatar had a political and social landscape similar to that of its neighbors across the Arab Gulf and inside the Gulf Cooperation Council (GCC). The singular ambition of the founders of QF was to build an institution that contributed to the development of the nation by advancing an agenda of social and educational development. In the almost 25 years since it was established, QF has evolved into a mosaic of many pieces, each unique in its own way but all connected by a belief in the role of education as the driver of all development. The sum of these parts represents a knowledge hub of committed and engaged faculty, researchers and students working together to maximize their potential for the benefit of Qatar and the wider region.

Even prior to the start of the crisis, the Foundation embodied a commitment to build a human and physical knowledge infrastructure unlike any in the region. In the process it had evolved into a successful educational model that other countries attempted to emulate in many ways. Since the blockade began, the Foundation has drawn on its standing as a bastion of diversity and a champion of tolerance and co-existence, to develop into something else, a differentiator between Qatar and its neighbors. The crisis has also served to bring the constituent parts of the Foundation together in the same unprecedented way as it has served to bring the constituent groups within wider Qatari society together over the same period.

On the practical level, the crisis has channeled QF to use its intellectual resources to offer a better understanding of events and to disseminate its findings across Qatari society through lectures, seminars, classroom discussions and more enduring projects such as this edited volume. Experts working at QF institutions have also played an important role in explaining the crisis to an interested global public via the international media by way of op-eds and commentaries, radio and television interviews, and public presentations in institutions across the world. In the course of all these undertakings, the Foundation has demonstrated its deeply personal and highly professional commitment to serve Qatar in its time of need on an intellectual and analytical level.

The crisis marked a paradigm shift in how Qatar saw itself in relation to its neighbors, who were also its long-time security and economic partners. The Foundation has also played a similarly important function since the start of the crisis. After the shock and anger of the initial weeks of the crisis, Qatar, its citizens and its residents increasingly began to see the crisis as an opportunity to achieve more independence and sustainability in many areas (from food security and defense, to the raw materials required for infrastructure projects, to the machinery and equipment needed across the country). This push toward greater self-sufficiency has also been evident in the educational sphere and there is no little pride among those who work for the Foundation, that its role as a leader in education, research, tolerance and peaceful co-existence has served as an important and influential source of soft power in this time of need.

Indeed, since the start of the crisis many senior figures in the Qatari government have pointed to the Foundation as a crucial contributor to the country's sustainability and development in the future. Its task of graduating Qatar's future business leaders, entrepreneurs, public officials and policymakers is more important now than it has ever been. Its role in conducting cutting-edge research in priority areas, including cyber security and food security, is more necessary than ever and in both of these two areas, QF entities have played a valuable supporting role in advising and providing analysis for the government.

The Foundation has also played an important role regionally and internationally during the crisis. Its commitment to innovation and the promotion of programs designed to popularize science, such as the "Stars of Science" program, encourage entrepreneurial young people to think about developing ideas and creations that could change the world. The Foundation has also sponsored forums and policy initiatives since the start of the crisis that have focused on other priority matters, which are a concern not only to Qatar but across the international community. Of particular note in this regard is the challenge of "fake news," something Qatar has been a victim of since the immediate period preceding the launch of the blockade. The World Innovation Summit for Education is held annually in Doha under the auspices of QF. In the first summit since the crisis began, in November 2017, some of the most important topics of discussions examined the ways to source credible information, and options for better educating students so that they ask the right questions and develop their critical thinking skills.

Currently, the Foundation has over 4,000 K-12 students and over 2,500 students in its affiliated higher education institutions. Students, faculty and staff have understood the value of QF during the blockade as a powerful force that can play a role in supporting Qatar in bringing its message to the world. Indeed, the Foundation's success in attracting foreign universities and maintaining deep strategic relationships with international academic leaders over decades is a source of real pride. These relationships have produced, and continue to produce, students qualified to give back to Qatari society. They have also elevated the standard of debate and intellectual life, as well as the nation's research priorities. The Foundation will continue to attract new students and faculty from all over the world, including the blockading countries, as a matter of course. In this and many other areas, the Foundation's long-term impact will be significant in eras of crisis and peace alike.

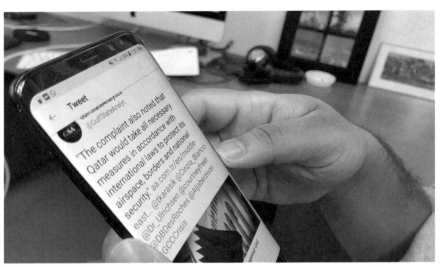

Section 2:

International Affairs

Qatar, the Gulf Crisis and Small State Behavior in International Affairs

RORY MILLER, GEORGETOWN UNIVERSITY IN QATAR

When Qatar entered the United Nations (UN) in the last few months of 1971, it was one of the world's smallest states. It was so small that its entry into the UN sparked a passionate debate in a period of decolonization over whether the international organization would have more credibility if it refused membership to such tiny nations. Almost half a century later, Qatar is still a small state when measured by traditional indicators – population, territory, military capability and, despite its oil and gas wealth, even GNP. But in recent decades its ambitious programs of state-branding and its standing as a key player in the global energy, financial, investment and property markets have seen it emerge as an actor of some significance in the international system.

So too has its pro-active and multidimensional diplomacy in the pre- and post-Arab Spring eras – in Darfur, Ethiopia and Eritrea, the Western Sahara, Libya and Tunisia, Lebanon, Palestine, Syria and Egypt and, closest to home, Yemen. This highly visible engagement on a number of fronts challenged the traditional view in the literature that small states are reactive and weak entities incapable of developing an independent foreign policy and of little importance in international affairs. As *The New York Times* put it in 2008, despite its size Qatar had managed to build a "bold new way to engage with the world while maintaining the country's independence."[1]

---

1   Robert F. Worth, 'Qatar, playing all sides, is a nonstop mediator,' *The New York Times*, 9 July 2008.

The current crisis has engendered a new debate over whether Qatar can counterbalance size-related difficulties to maintain political autonomy, diplomatic influence and economic sovereignty in a hostile security environment. In doing so, it has also re-ignited a more general debate over the role and power of small states in the international system. In early July 2017, the eminent Singaporean diplomat and former UN Security Council President, Kishore Mahbubani, penned a widely read article claiming that Qatar had, to some degree, brought the crisis on itself by too often ignoring the "eternal rule of geopolitics: small states must behave like small states."[1] Writing a few weeks later, James M. Dorsey, a respected Gulf commentator, presented another perspective. Qatar's response to the blockade, he argued, as well as the role of the United Arab Emirates (UAE) on the other side of the conflict, was not evidence of weakness but rather marked the "coming out of small states capable of punching far above their weight."[2] Speaking in the midst of the current crisis, at the Munich Security Conference in February 2018, Qatar's amir made a similar point. He argued that the "failed blockade," demonstrated "how small states can use diplomacy and strategic economic planning to weather the storms of aggression from larger, ambitious neighbors."[3]

It is too early to tell whether Qatar's response to the current crisis will ultimately serve as a warning or a model for other small states surrounded by much larger threatening foes who are committed to their diplomatic and economic isolation. But the Qatari experience so far does help us better understand the options available to small states, and the challenges that they will invariably face, in attempting to overcome similar difficulties in the future.

Size, Capabilities and Foreign Policy

Size is a very important consideration in international affairs because surplus capabilities on the national level are a key determinant of a state's

---

1   Kishore Mahbubani, 'Qatar: Big lessons from a small country,' *Strait Times*, 1 July 2017.

2   James M. Dorsey, 'The Gulf Crisis: A coming out of small states,' *Commandeleven*, 14 July 2017, www.commandeleven.com

3   'Speech of Qatar Emir at Munich Security Conference,' *The Peninsula Qatar*, 16 February 2018, https://thepeninsulaqatar.com/article/16/02/2018/Speech-of-Qatar-Emir-at-Munich-Security-Conference.

security and external influence. The best, and perhaps most obvious, example is the United States' status as the dominant global military power. This is a consequence of many factors, including, not least, an annual military budget greater than that of China, Russia, the United Kingdom, France, Japan, Saudi Arabia and India combined. This is only possible because of the size of the US economy, which means that the $600 billion a year Washington spends on maintaining its military pre-eminence still only accounts for around 3.5% of total GDP.

The current Gulf crisis is a classic case of conflict between a small state and a major power. The four core members of the anti-Qatar coalition – Saudi Arabia, the UAE, Egypt and Bahrain – have a combined population that is 55 times bigger than Qatar's (137 million compared to 2.5 million); they control a combined territory that is 279 times larger than the State of Qatar (3,234 million km² compared with 11,571 km²), with Saudi Arabia alone, 186 times bigger than its besieged neighbor; their combined military spending, based on 2015 figures, is 16 times greater than Qatar's ($112,871 billion compared to $7 billion); while their combined GNP, also based on 2015 figures, is 11 times greater ($3.5 trillion compared to $309 billion).

On one level, this massive disparity in conventional power does give weight to Mahbubani's argument that small states must "exercise discretion" and be "restrained on matters involving great powers."[1] Realist thinkers, who almost always equate smallness with weakness, would agree with this assessment by the veteran Singaporean statesman. This was also the consensus view among the group of influential thinkers who developed the small states literature between the late 1960s and early 1980s, in the shadow of rapid decolonization and at the height of a superpower Cold War between the Soviet Union and the United States. This literature argued the following about small states:

- They are far more sensitive than larger powers to changes in the external environment and those changes will have a greater impact on small states because they do not have the physical capabilities or resources to fend off external threats.
- They understand their own vulnerabilities, especially their

---

1   Kishore Mahbubani, 'Qatar: Big lessons from a small country,' *Strait Times*, 1 July 2017.

limited capacity to move beyond foreign engagement that is both reactive and involuntary.

- Their awareness of this causes them to be more preoccupied than bigger actors with immediate security concerns and their own survival and often results in them joining alliances to gain the protection of more powerful partners.

Though not discounting the importance of size, more recent scholarship rejects the traditionally negative view of small state capabilities and does not automatically accept that there exist structural preconditions for power as much of the earlier literature suggested. Instead, this body of work argues that:

- There is no consistent correlation between traditional size-based indicators of power (population, military strength and wealth) and a small state's viability in the international system.
- Domestic unity is a vital factor in the security and stability of a state and, as such, elites in small states may find it easier than those in bigger powers to promote societal cooperation, the building of new institutions, and the initiation of political and economic reform in the face of external threats.
- "Smallness" can contribute positively to the construction of state identities that can facilitate innovative foreign as well as domestic policies.

Testing Small State Assumptions in the Gulf Crisis

One can find evidence of both traditional and more recent thinking on how small states respond to external threats in Qatari behavior in both the pre- and post-blockade eras. In the pre-blockade era, Qatar's social cohesion and "smallness" provided the domestic unity that made possible the country's most significant branding and investment decisions. This was true for Al Jazeera, the prized cable news network that was launched in 1996 to "help put tiny Qatar on the map,"[1] as then Amir, Sheikh Hamad bin Khalifa Al Thani, explained at the time. These factors also explain Qatar's success in becoming the smallest country to ever bid for, and win, the right to host

---

1   Norbert Wildermuth, 'Defining the "Al-Jazeera Effect": American Public Diplomacy at a Crossroad,' *Media Res*, Vol. 1, No. 2 (February 2005).

FIFA's soccer World Cup, as well as the first Muslim and Middle Eastern country to be chosen to stage the world's biggest sporting event. These same positive small state characteristics also empowered a pro-active and visionary foreign policy elite to introduce innovative strategies that scored important diplomatic victories over much stronger opponents.

However, the availability of surplus material capabilities, in particular financial resources, were also central to Qatar's pursuit of an ambitious foreign policy agenda in the pre-blockade era. Qatar's mastery of "riyal politic,"[1] as one astute commentator has described the country's use of gas revenues to fund its external engagement, is a case in point. Prior to the current crisis, this was central to Qatar's success in mediating between Fatah and Hamas in Palestine following the latter's rise to power in Gaza in 2006. It was also a key factor in Lebanon where a Qatari-sponsored peace proposal succeeded in bringing the opposing factions to the negotiating table despite the previous failure of major players like the United States and Saudi Arabia to achieve the same. Financial diplomacy also played a significant role for Qatar in its conflict resolution efforts in Yemen and Darfur and in its interventions in Libya, Egypt and Syria during and since the Arab Spring.

Small states have traditionally entered into alliances with larger powers or have relied heavily on their protection to obtain security from external threats. Qatar's success in establishing such relationships in the pre-blockade era also played an important role in its evolution into a key regional diplomatic player. The most important of these was Qatar's embrace of the United States as a key pillar of its security and defense doctrine. From the late 1990s, Qatar invested heavily in consolidating and expanding this relationship as part of its long-term goal of stability at home and security and influence outside of its borders.

Its success in finding security "shelter" in the bilateral alliance with Washington, combined with its diplomatic achievements in the wider Arab and Muslim world, generated tensions and jealousies among those local actors who viewed Qatar's independent foreign policy as an obstacle to

---

1   Abdulla Baabood, 'Dynamics and Determinants of the GCC States' Foreign Policy, with Special Reference to the EU,' in Gerd Nonneman (ed.), *Analyzing Middle East Foreign Policies and the Relationship with Europe*, London and New York: Routledge, 2005, pp. 145–173.

their own strategic ambitions, not to mention a challenge to their political and ideological visions for the wider Middle East. In these terms, the current crisis can be understood primarily as a function of competition between ambitious neighbors for regional influence in an increasingly interconnected international system. But this crisis is also a function of "smallness." Qatar's rise to international prominence became increasingly intolerable for elites in Saudi Arabia, Egypt and the UAE, who respectively considered their own states to be the dominant big power actors and the dominant "small state" actor in the Arab system.

This is particularly the case for Saudi Arabia, which has the Arab Gulf's biggest economy, population, oil reserves and army and, as noted above, a territory that is 186 times larger than Qatar. Saudi elites have always exhibited deeply held feelings of cultural and religious, as well as political, superiority toward their smaller neighbors, including Qatar, in a region where traditional identities and hierarchies have always been, and still remain, a source of power and legitimacy.

In many ways, today's crisis stems from these tensions, which are as much historical and ideational as geopolitical in nature. In the modern era, this played out following the establishment of Saudi Arabia in the early 1930s, when the kingdom's founder, Abdulaziz ibn Saud, attempted to claim large parts of Qatar for his kingdom. Since then, and especially after independence in 1971, Qatar has had to defend its sovereignty and territorial integrity from Saudi encroachment, and has also been involved in several territorial disputes with Bahrain and the UAE, both of whom also gained their independence at the start of the 1970s.

These tensions boiled over in the summer of 1995 when Saudi Arabia, supported by Bahrain and the UAE, attempted to undermine the rise to power of Qatar's new amir, Sheikh Hamad bin Khalifa Al Thani. Prior to becoming amir, Sheikh Hamad had demonstrated a willingness to stand up to his larger neighbor and this failed intervention shaped the kingdom's evolving foreign policy approach. Over the next two decades, Qatar's rising wealth and status challenged Saudi diplomatic and political dominance and the UAE's more recent efforts to turn its status as the Gulf's top trading and communications hub into geo-strategic influence.

This dynamic was greatly exacerbated by perceptions of "smallness" among the different actors. Qatar did not see any reason why its tiny population and territory or its lack of military might should be barriers to an independent foreign policy or regional influence. Saudi Arabia and the UAE disagreed. This explains why, in March 2014, Saudi Arabia, the UAE and Bahrain recalled their ambassadors from Doha and, in a brief foretaste of what was to come, threatened to implement sanctions against their GCC partner. This unprecedented coordinated diplomatic boycott was intended to send a clear message to Doha that its divergent policies in Syria, Egypt and Libya, and its approach toward Iran and the Muslim Brotherhood, would no longer be tolerated by the bigger powers in the Gulf.

It also explains why the attacks on Qatar since the start of the blockade in June 2017 have not only targeted the tiny country's foreign policy, airspace, borders and economy but also transcended Western conceptions of sovereignty and the nation-state by challenging its legitimacy and history. Once this is understood it makes it easier to see why the list of grievances issued by the anti-Qatar coalition in late June 2017 made no concessions to Qatari sovereign rights and instead read like the demands of a medieval feudal lord dealing with an insubordinate vassal.

Since the start of the crisis, Qatar has contained the negative impact of isolation and blockade better than many states with larger populations, territories or even economies would have done. While searching for a *modus vivendi* with the blockading countries it has also effectively used its soft power and diplomacy to consolidate existing relationships and build new ones across the international community to meet the external threats it now faces from former GCC partners. This has resulted in a rapidly expanding military and security relationship with Turkey, which has led to the opening of a Turkish military base in Qatar. As Qatar's Minister of State for Defense and Deputy Prime Minister, Khalid bin Mohammad Al Attiyah, explained at a meeting in London in January 2018, this is a "strategic partnership to enhance and diversify [Qatar's] defense capabilities."[1]

The crisis has also pushed Qatar closer to Iran, which sees the crisis as an opportunity to, among other things, undermine Saudi Arabia, its regional nemesis. Prior to the blockade, Turkey and Qatar had positive relations. Qatar's relationship with Iran over the years has been much more

---

1   'A Conversation with Qatar Defence Minister H.E. Dr. Khalid Bin Mohammad Al Attiyah,' Royal United Services Institute (RUSI), 17 January 2018. https://rusi.org/event/conversation-qatar-defence-minister-he-dr-khalid-bin-mohammad-al-attiyah

ambiguous. With the exception of Oman, Qatar has backed engagement and dialogue with Iran more than any of its GCC partners. This is a function of history, geography, small state vulnerabilities and economic interest, especially as Qatar shares with Iran its largest gas field – the North-West Dome (North Field) off its northeast coast. But until the current crisis it had resisted Iranian overtures to break with the Saudi-led Sunni Gulf and had instead regularly backed GCC condemnations of Iranian foreign policy, and joined the Saudi-led Yemen coalition and the Islamic Military Alliance, both of which prioritized the Iranian threat.

Rising relations with Turkey and Iran during the crisis served the security interests of Qatar by providing a balance to the hard power threat posed by Saudi Arabia and the UAE on its borders. Iran and Turkey also contributed to the consolidation of Qatari economic and political sovereignty by facilitating, often in cooperation with each other, Qatar's vital efforts to access airspace, open up new trade routes and import necessary supplies.

Conclusion and Lessons Learned

After the initial shock caused by the scale and severity of the blockade, Qatar quickly moved out of survival mode and succeeded in achieving its priority objective – protecting its sovereignty and retaining political and economic autonomy. In doing so, the country once more challenged the traditional conception of national security simply and solely as a function of military power and territorial size. Since the crisis began, Qatar has also demonstrated repeatedly that a small, culturally homogeneous state with a strong national identity and a popular leader can achieve the unity required to withstand pressure from much stronger external threats.

On the other hand, throughout the crisis, Qatar has had to draw on its significant financial resources to stave off the worst consequences of economic isolation and blockade. This fact underscores how problematic it is to generalize about the relevance of one small state's experience for others, as few small states have Qatar's financial reserves at their disposal to address the external threats that they face. The current crisis also demonstrates the extent, as the traditional literature suggests, that surplus capabilities, in this case financial ones, are a vital component in the arsenal of small states under intense external pressure because they allow for economic self-reliance at home.

Similarly, Qatar's search for new allies to balance the threat posed by the much more powerful coalition ranged against it also gives credence to the traditional view in the literature that small states generally require a powerful protector when challenged by larger neighbors. It is too early to know whether closer ties with Turkey and Iran might lead to the erosion of national sovereignty, security or political dependence. It should be noted that in the past Qatar has managed to defy the conventional patterns of a patron-client relationship while involved in alliances with Saudi Arabia inside the GCC and the United States on the bilateral level. In both these cases, Qatar successfully pursued its own security interests even when then they ran counter to the priorities or interests of these two more powerful partners. In the American case, this was evident in the way the leadership in Doha adopted, at little cost, positions on a number of foreign policy issues, such as supporting Hamas in Palestine, that infuriated Washington.

In conclusion, the disparity in size and resources between Qatar and the blockading countries means that, despite its impressive soft power capabilities, Qatar is vulnerable if the status quo continues into the longer term. This explains why Qatar has consistently sought diplomatic solutions to the conflict and why it attempted to find imaginative ways to reconfigure existing alliance dynamics so that the leaderships in Abu Dhabi and Riyadh (and to a lesser extent Cairo) feel the political cost of maintaining the blockade. While this is difficult to achieve, Qatar's response to the crisis so far has demonstrated that a small state, even an isolated one located in a highly unstable regional setting, can overcome the limitations of size and capabilities in the short and medium term, as long as it has the domestic social cohesion and the available financial resources required to deal with the challenges it faces in a pro-active and innovative manner.

The Qatar Crisis through the Lens of Foreign Policy Analysis

GERD NONNEMAN, GEORGETOWN UNIVERSITY IN QATAR

The Qatar crisis presents the sorts of questions Foreign Policy Analysis would seem well suited to help answer. The most obvious derives from the extent to which the blockading countries' approach, in its sudden, far-reaching and seemingly impetuous nature, appeared to diverge in key respects from past foreign policy patterns in the Gulf. At the same time, the case study may illuminate aspects of this sub-discipline of International Relations.

Approaches in Foreign Policy Analysis

Different approaches in Foreign Policy Analysis[1] prioritize different factors as likely determinants of foreign policy output. Some focus on the explanation of particular decisions, others on broader patterns of output. In both cases the sorts of categories considered include environmental factors both at the system level and at the domestic level; factors at the level of decision-making actors and the role and dynamics of bureaucracies; cognitive theories and political psychology; and the personalities/types of leaders.

The international environment as a factor is viewed differently by different schools of thought. "Realists" prioritize the pursuit of power aimed at survival in an anarchic international system; for "defensive realists" a state will try to maintain its relative power position amidst a given

---

1   A user-friendly summary of these different approaches can be found in Derek Beach, *Analyzing Foreign Policy*, New York: Palgrave Macmillan, 2012, pp. 34–61.

balance of threats, with the immediate focus on protection against the state seen as the greatest threat (given intent, capabilities and proximity); "offensive realists" see states as trying to *increase* their power, possibly to try and achieve regional hegemony. "Liberals" emphasize *interdependence* (economic and otherwise) at the systemic level; some "liberal institutionalists" also believe that within the anarchic system, the impact of international institutions on states' assumptions, options and behaviors can nevertheless be significant. Finally, "constructivists" argue that ideational factors are as important as material ones since the latter only take on meaning through actors' collective understanding: the international system is socially constructed, or as Wendt put it, "anarchy is what states make of it."[1]

"Structural realists" have relatively little interest in what goes on inside the black box of domestic politics and decision-making. Among liberals and constructivists there is a greater willingness to accept that it is important to consider what goes on at the domestic level in order to arrive at a more fine-grained understanding of policy outcomes. Among realists, too, a "neo-classical" school emerged which recognized that state-level factors are important to understand actual tangible policy choices and outcomes.

The domestic environment includes such factors as the nature of the political system; the nature and extent of wider societal debates (public opinion) and influence on policy; national political culture(s); and the impact of "elite" public opinion and interest groups such as lobbyists, politicians, think tanks and the media.

Of course, the purely material factors – within and across borders – that tend to be privileged by realists should also be considered. These include geographic location, demography, economic development, industrial capacity and military strength. Yet in the view of neoclassical realists, liberals and constructivists alike, these are not simply givens in their own right: they are interpreted by state-level actors as part of their assumptions about their and their states' interests.

The study of the way in which actual decision-making then occurs against this background, is what the sub-discipline of Foreign Policy Analysis has been most associated with: it is here that bureaucratic politics,

---

1   Alexander Wendt, 'Anarchy is what states make of it: the social construction of international politics,' *International Organization*, Vol. 46, No. 2 (1992), pp. 391–425.

group dynamics, cognitive and psychological factors and leadership traits come in.

It is possible to discern certain role conceptions that come to character-ize states' foreign policies: a set of views of their and their countries' position and proper role in the region and the world. These role conceptions are influenced by the longer-term experience of the country's (and perhaps the leading group's) path; by understandings of the nature of regional and inter-national politics; and by societal factors, norms and political culture. In turn, they inform how particular situations, threats and opportunities are viewed and acted on. By definition they have a longer-term character, therefore, but that does not mean they are immutable: it is conceivable that a different generation of leadership – or indeed a different political group or individual leader – may have views, perceptions and inclinations that trans-late into a shift in role conception.

Patterns in Gulf States' Foreign Policies

Despite their hydrocarbon resources, financial wealth and impressive military hardware, the six Gulf Cooperation Council (GCC) states have remained vulnerable in other ways, both as states and as regimes. Saudi Arabia apart, they are small and without much, if any, strategic depth; they have small national populations; and their militaries (with the very recent exception of the UAE) are far less potent than their hardware suggests, both because of manpower challenges and their limited ability to operate and maintain this hardware independently. They have long faced a number of strategic and ideological regional threats, not least those emanating from Iran and Iraq.

The five smaller GCC states have also faced an additional threat in the form of Saudi Arabia – which not only dwarfs them but grew out of a polity whose leadership since the 19th century had ambitions of territorial or trib-utary dominance over territories now included in their sovereign states.

In structural realist terms, then, all these states, including Saudi Arabia, could be expected to prioritize their survival and maximize their power both by building up their own military capabilities and, more importantly, by align-ing themselves with major powers who could offer protection. Such outside protection would help allow a state like Saudi Arabia to "balance" against Iran and Iraq, in order to maintain its relative power position in the system.

For the smaller states, a collective "balancing" might be conceivable both by banding together – as in the case of the GCC – and by anchoring their security ultimately in great power protection. In regard to relations with Saudi Arabia, they arguably face a choice between "balancing" and "bandwagoning." Bahrain by and large opted for the latter, as it became strategically and economically dependent on its giant neighbor. The others tried to walk a fine line between both options – enabled by the guarantee of US protection. Only Qatar has opted, since 1995, more explicitly for the "balancing" option – albeit one diplomatically attenuated in various ways, including through its membership in the GCC, its decision not to obstruct the Saudi operation in support of the Bahraini regime in 2011, and its restrained participation in the Saudi-Emirati Yemen operation that was launched in 2015.

Yet these calculations were not merely about state security: they were at least as much about regime security. Indeed, in these states the ruling family regimes are very much integral to the conception and current nature of the state. In all except Oman, the current ruling family was at the origin of the creation of these political entities; Oman's current dynasty has been in power since the mid-18th century.

Neither was the exercise of power and the formation of policy formalized and bureaucratized in the way much FPA theorizing assumes: individuals and intra-family groups mattered and put their security from internal, as well as external, threats at the center. The way in which these individuals interpreted and responded to their perceived threat environment, therefore, was very much shaped not only by material factors, but by their own mental make-up, history and proclivities. Leaders, in other words, matter – even if they are constrained by the sorts of material environmental factors and capabilities that realists might focus on.

When observing the foreign policy of these six states over the past century or more, it is also clear that there are common patterns of behavior, because of a combination of similar threat and resource environments, mutual learning, and traits deriving from local political culture.[1] The ways

---

1 For a summing-up of the broad dynamics of GCC states' foreign policies, see Abdulla Baabood, 'Dynamics and Determinants of the GCC States' Foreign Policy,' in Gerd Nonneman (ed.), *Analyzing Middle East Foreign Policies, and the Relationship with Europe*, London and New York: Routledge, 2005, pp. 145–173.

in which these leaders since the end of the 19th century have interpreted
and dealt with their material environment, but also with the ideological
threat component of that environment, seems most readily compatible with
elements of the neoclassical, liberal and constructivist approaches. It shows
the importance (as the case of the Qatar crisis will show) of individual
leaders' particular personalities, predilections and worldviews. It also illus-
trates the importance of the political system and decision-making structures
for understanding policy choices.

Those patterns have included a determination to attract the hegemon of
the day as one's main protector while combining this with a concerted
attempt to develop complementary relationships, not least to help reel in
and keep close the hegemon, while simultaneously making clear that they
were not to be taken for granted.

Dynastic competition including armed clashes between the different
ruling families over influence and territory was a regular feature and, in the
case of the nine Trucial states, often linked to intra-family competition. But
at least after Kuwait's success in the 1920 battle of Jahra against the Al
Saud's attempted encroachment, there was also always a determination, in
line with Arabian tribal and sheikhly norms and in part in acknowledgement that the ruling families' interests were ultimately served by restraint,
to keep open channels of communication and retreat. This offered ways of
saving face and honor and safeguarded avenues for de-escalation. As a
result, the social and kinship fabric between different parts of the Gulf and
between various ruling families, was never damaged beyond repair. This
fundamental pragmatism is a common pattern over the last century.

A long-term view also allows one to discern the role conceptions inherent in the foreign policies of these states and these ruling families. The Al
Saud's role conception has always included its status as the dominant player
in the Arabian Peninsula. Dubai's role conception has been based on an
openness to the world, pragmatism and the a-political engagement of
commercial opportunities. Oman's role conception has long included an
openness to the wider world, a reluctance to be too tightly bound to the
Arab world and, under Sultan Qaboos, a pragmatic tendency to serve as a
mediator in regional disputes.

At the heart of Abu Dhabi's role conception was a land-based power
combined with a self-perception of fighting prowess and sheikhly wisdom,
not to mention a strong sense of its senior status among the Trucial states,

long before it became oil-rich. Qatar's role conception clearly changed following the accession to power of the highly ambitious and confident Sheikh Hamad in 1995: from a low-profile actor with limited ambitions beyond security in its early decades after independence, the country, fueled by gas revenues, a strong self-belief and a determination to earn international respect, was soon a pro-active regional diplomatic player with a growing global reputation.

The Case of the Qatar Crisis

The 2014 diplomatic spat between Qatar and Saudi Arabia, Bahrain and the UAE, was in some ways just the latest phase in a long-running story. Part of it was the old dynastic and territorial rivalry between the Al Thani and the Al Khalifa of Bahrain. It was also in part a consequence of a long-standing political issue with Riyadh and Abu Dhabi, both of whom had been sympathetic to a coup attempt against Sheikh Hamad in 1996, a year after he had taken power from his father. This reinforced Sheikh Hamad's conviction that Saudi Arabia was the primary threat to Qatar's sovereignty and his own leadership. His foreign policy henceforth doubled down on ways to secure his regime and Qatar by locking in US protection, including by granting use of the Al-Udhaid airbase. At the same time, Qatari defense procurement has reflected a conscious choice to nurture strong complementary relationships – not least with France and Britain.

The start of the Arab Spring in 2011, just months after Qatar became the world's number one exporter of liquefied natural gas (LNG), provided an opportunity for it to use all available instruments of national power, notably its great wealth and the Al Jazeera news network, to play an even more proactive role on the regional scene, which would serve to underscore its difference and consolidate its independence.

Qatar's support for the wave of popular opposition – including the Muslim Brotherhood – exacerbated the concerns of the leaderships in Abu Dhabi, Riyadh and Bahrain by challenging their regional dominance and enabling a potential alternative narrative to their preferred "authentic Arabian governance" model of authoritarian stability. Even so, it proved possible to find a face-saving way to calm the spat – as the previous century's experience suggested would be the case.

The 2017 Qatar crisis, although partly rooted in the same dynamics, was different. The blockading countries immediately escalated disagreements to the gravest level short of military action. As soon became evident, this left no room for ratcheting up pressure if "Plan A" failed. Nor was a clear set of demands evident from the outset, and when those demands were finally issued they were so maximalist and unrealistic that it appeared to observers that they were intended to fail.

As a result, the old conventions of safeguarding a means of compromise, retreat, face-saving and de-escalation were discarded; so were socio-cultural norms relating to the way that ruling families engaged with each other. Instead, explicit support was given to the legitimacy of regime change in the case of Qatar, and the social fabric tying Qatar into the rest of Gulf society was ripped up in ways that promise to leave deep scars. Pragmatism – a defining characteristic of the foreign policies of the Gulf states for over a century – was abandoned and with it went the viability of the GCC as an effective regional economic and security forum.

What explains this change in long-standing patterns, and the seemingly ill-advised tools chosen to achieve the anti-Qatar coalition's presumed aims?

First, the decision-making environment in Saudi Arabia and the UAE has changed significantly. A decade earlier, I would argue, the domestic situations in both countries would never have resulted in pre-existing disagreements and frictions with Qatar leading to such radical action. The UAE was a confederation, in which Dubai retained relative autonomy vis-à-vis federal policies, including on foreign affairs. In Saudi Arabia, multiple princes oversaw their own portfolios, a reality that required caution, compromise and conciliation at the highest levels of the Saudi ruling family.

With the consolidation of power by Crown Prince Mohammed bin Salman (known as MBS), including his move to eliminate alternative power centers, generations of experience and strong external networks were lost: all significant decisions on foreign policy are now taken by an inexperienced crown prince and a small group of his closest advisors, whose first imperative is to abet their ruler's wishes.

In the UAE, two things combined to alter the decision-making environment. The first was the rising confidence of Abu Dhabi's Crown Prince Mohammed bin Zayed (known as MBZ) as the memory of his father, the federation's pragmatic and magnanimous founding President Sheikh Zayed, faded. Second, Abu Dhabi's role in providing financial relief to a near-bankrupt Dubai during the 2008 global financial crisis ensured that Dubai in effect lost its autonomy, including in foreign and security policy. MBZ and a small group of courtiers now determine the UAE's foreign policy as a whole.

It also seems clear that Saudi Arabia's crown prince looks to his Abu Dhabi counterpart as something of a mentor and their mutual admiration and reinforcement (with the older MBZ initially in the lead), were also important drivers of the form the crisis took.

Second, in this changed decision-making environment, the personalities of leaders acquire added importance. The key decisions were made by two men who are by all accounts impatient and headstrong, have a limited tolerance for contrary opinions, and are imbued with a sense of their, and their state's, leadership mission in the Arabian Peninsula.

Moreover, MBZ is known to be steeped in, and to view things through the prism of, the military and security establishment: having been nurtured in this environment from youth, he made it central to his political development project for the UAE. His attitude toward the Muslim Brotherhood or *any* model of governance at variance with his recipe for a political framework both at home and in the wider region, must be seen in that light.

Third, the above derived added importance from the significant improvement in the UAE's security and military capabilities in recent years, which have provided the *material* basis for the changing role conception.

Fourth, these changing role conceptions in Riyadh and Abu Dhabi, a consequence of the three factors addressed above, directly explain the unprecedented levels of confidence and proactive regional engagement among key decision-makers in the UAE and Saudi Arabia.

The *fifth* factor is to be found in the external environment, where Donald Trump, the new US president, was viewed by decision-makers in Riyadh and Abu Dhabi as a crucial potential ally. At least initially this proved correct and it is unlikely, absent such a belief, that the decision to move against Qatar in such a zero-sum manner would have been made.

Conclusion and Lessons Learned

The Gulf crisis demonstrates clearly that the foreign policies of regional states, including those of small and vulnerable states, are not determined simply by relative power in the regional, or even global, system. While calculations of regime and state security in a context of the overall material and ideational threat environment are central, we should also note a number of other important points.

First, this calculation is made by individual leaders whose interpretations and decisions are not constrained by bureaucratic foreign policy apparatuses except in the sense that the filtering and assessment of information and options that take place in more developed foreign policy settings is largely absent here, while the capability for implementation and follow-through when policy meets the complexities of the environment it is meant to impact, is more limited.

Second, these calculations and decisions *are* shaped (though not determined) by existing role conceptions, world views, and the individual mental make-up and idiosyncrasies of the leaders concerned. Changes in the top decision-making echelons – both in terms of people and of the particular power structures they inhabit – are therefore important factors.

Third, these state leaderships make policy as "omibalancers," on the basis of an assessment of where the main threats – whether material or ideational, domestic or external – to their overall security reside.[1]

Some of these states do exhibit behaviors that match the expectations of "offensive realism" in the sense that they attempt proactively to increase their relative power position in the regional environment. This seems true of Saudi Arabia and Abu Dhabi. Arguably Qatar did something similar through its use of soft power and the prioritization of external resources and support up to 2013, though since then its approach has been less ambitious and more defensive.

Constructivist insights would appear to be of obvious relevance in highlighting the ideational aspects of policy-making, including the fact that the regional system's features are as much a function of world views and perceptions among the various leaderships as of given material hard facts.

The liberal school is relevant especially given its emphasis on interdependence (not least economic) as a factor that shapes options, attitudes and constraints. Its institutionalist variant draws our attention to state actors' use of UN institutions, and to the intermittent, if decreasingly significant,

---

1   For the main exposition on the concept of "omnibalancing," see Steven David, 'Explaining Third World Alignment,' *World Politics*, Vol. 43, No. 2 (1991), pp. 233–256.

use of such fora as the Arab League. The liberal prism is also useful for reflecting on the nature, uses and impact of the GCC. Even though the organization is unlikely to recover, it unquestionably had an important impact on the perceptions of the regional environment and even identity for two generations of Gulf citizens and decision-makers. This is not something that will disappear easily or quickly. Indeed, while the GCC framework is unlikely to ever again determine the policy choices of individual Gulf states, after almost four decades in existence, the institution has left a mark on social consciousness across the Gulf. The ways in which this might influence future perceptions and policy remain to be seen.

In any case, all six GCC states have continued the pattern of seeking to anchor their security in the protection of the hegemon of the day (for the foreseeable future the US), while expanding and deepening their relationships with other actors. The context of relative shifts in the global power landscape has enabled a more forceful demonstration than was usually the norm in the past, of relative autonomy from major powers in the determination of policy preferences.[1] The spectacle of the anti-Qatar coalition ignoring the blandishments of a US secretary of state to resolve the crisis was a striking illustration. Yet at the same time, that autonomy remains relative, constrained as it is by these same states' ultimate dependence on US and Western security guarantees as well as military, technological and economic relations.

Conversely, Qatar has demonstrated the effectiveness of its combined strategy of anchoring its security to the US while nurturing an extensive network of complementary relationships. At the same time, it also discovered the limitations of using soft power as an equalizer in the power balance with its neighbors. These stemmed from a combination of relatively limited foreign policy "machinery" capabilities, the complexities of the political landscape it was engaging with, and the material facts of relative size and geographic position. This became evident in, arguably, some overreach during the more ambitious early phase of its Arab Spring enthusiasm, with

---

1   I have developed this notion of "relative autonomy" in a more in-depth manner in the case of Middle Eastern states generally, in 'Analyzing the Foreign Policies of the Middle East and North Africa: A Conceptual Framework', in Gerd Nonneman (ed.), *Analyzing Middle East Foreign Policies, and the Relationship with Europe*, London and New York: Routledge, 2005, pp. 6–18.

at times inadequate "due diligence" in identifying partners, and insufficient alternative scenario planning and follow-up. Yet in the final analysis, it has been able to secure its economic and political survival.

Cyber Security in Qatar and the Gulf Crisis

JOSEPH J. BOUTROS, TEXAS A&M UNIVERSITY AT QATAR

Cyber or computer security, one of the most pressing issues of our times, deals with the protection of computer systems[1] from theft and damage; it includes the study of operating systems security, malware (viruses), web security and network security.

The security of computer systems and the internet in Qatar is vital to maintaining a prosperous economy and guaranteeing a safe environment for the country's population, which faces potential cyber attacks from individuals (hackers), organizations, or states intent on stealing, altering, or destroying targeted data by hacking into a computer system.

Fundamentals of Cyber Security

Secure systems depend on the six pillars of *Information Assurance* in cyber security. The first three concepts are known as the CIA triad: C for confidentiality, I for integrity, and A for availability. According to the National Information Assurance Glossary (NIAG),[2] confidentiality is the assurance that information is not disclosed to unauthorized individuals,

---

1 The number of internet hosts has exceeded 1 billion in 2018 and the number of smartphones approaches 3 billion.

2 *National Information Assurance Glossary*, National Security Telecommunications and Information Systems Security Committee, NSTISSI No. 4009, US, April 2010.

processes, or devices and primarily focuses on protecting information.[1] Integrity in cyber security is to ensure that stored data are accurate and contain no unauthorized modifications. Keys to maintaining integrity are authentication, a security measure designed to establish the validity of a transmission or originator, or a means of verifying an individual's authorization to receive specific categories of information; authorization is the privileged access granted to a specific user, program or process; and nonrepudiation, which is proof to the sender that data is delivered and proof to the recipient of the sender's identity, so neither can later deny having processed the data. The final requirement is availability, defined as timely and reliable access to data and information services for authorized users.

The Qatar Case Study

In the past three years, Qatar's Ministry of Transport and Telecommunications dealt with an estimated 2,000 cyber incidents and processed 851 million files with security threats, including 3.7 million virus infections. The table below, with sources from Qatar's Ministry of Interior, shows how the number of reports for electronic crimes increased from 2011 to 2016.[2]

Year	2011	2012	2013	2014	2015	2016
Number of filed reports for electronic crimes	169	204	324	429	643	1,105

Such an increase may reflect two joint phenomena: that the number of cyber crimes is increasing in Qatar with the widespread adoption of connected devices and computers, and that the Ministry of Interior is improving its capabilities in detecting and reporting these cyber crimes. From November 2016 to October 2017, Kaspersky Lab calculated how

---

1   The three principal confidentiality aims are: (1) Information must have protections capable of preventing some users from accessing it, (2) Limitations must be in place to restrict access to the information to only those who have the authorization to view it, (3) An authentication system must be in place to verify the identity of those with access to the data.

2   Qatar's 2nd National Development Strategy, Doha, March 2018.

often users encountered detection verdicts on their machines in 2017. The resulting data characterize the risk of infection as shown below. As one can see, in this Kaspersky Lab analysis Qatar was held to face a medium risk with 34.2% of users attacked.

Country	Level of risk	% users attacked (online infection)
Algeria	High risk group	44.06
Belarus	Medium risk group	38.39
Russia	Medium risk group	36.91
Tunisia	Medium risk group	36.51
Vietnam	Medium risk group	35.01
Qatar	Medium risk group	34.20
Brazil	Medium risk group	32.66
United States	Low risk group	19.40
Japan	Low risk group	15.41
Ireland	Low risk group	12.15

Security of the Internet Backbone

The map shows the six fiber-optic submarine cables connecting the State of Qatar to the internet. These cables are listed in the table below.

A cyber vulnerability is found in all fiber-optic cables linking Qatar with the outside world. Indeed, all six listed submarine cables go through a neighboring country. The

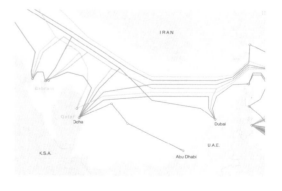

Qatar-UAE cable has a unique socket in Abu-Dhabi. FOG goes to Kuwait but it has sockets in Bahrain and the UAE. Falcon has a socket in Fujairah before leaving the UAE. Similar weaknesses are found in the remaining cables. The most recent, AAE-1, has a socket in Fujairah (UAE) before entering the Indian Ocean to reach other countries.

Name of submarine fiber optic cable	Ready For Service (RFS)	Length (kms)	Connected Countries
Fiber Optic Gulf (FOG)	June 1998	1,300	Qatar, UAE, Bahrain, Kuwait
Qatar-UAE submarine cable	Dec. 2004	100	Qatar, UAE
Falcon	Sept. 2006	10,300	Yemen, Saudi Arabia, UAE, Kuwait, Oman, Iraq, Iran, Qatar, Bahrain, India, Sudan, Egypt
Tata TGN-Gulf	Feb. 2012	4,031	Qatar, Bahrain, UAE, Saudi Arabia, Oman
Gulf Bridge International Cable System (GBICS)	Feb. 2012	5,000	Qatar, Bahrain, Saudi Arabia, Iraq, Iran, Kuwait, UAE, Oman, India
Asia Africa Europe AAE-1	June 2017	25,000	Qatar, UAE, Oman, Yemen, Saudi Arabia, Djibouti, Egypt, India, Pakistan, Cambodia, Myanmar, Thailand, Vietnam, Malaysia, Hong Kong, Greece, Italy, France

Clearly, the cyber vulnerability we are pointing to here in relation to these submarine cables may threaten the availability and the confidentiality of international communications from and to Qatar. In the worst-case scenario of a regional crisis that is militarized, for example, all cables connecting Qatar to the internet could potentially be cut at Fujairah. In a less extreme scenario, it may be possible to listen in on some communications at sockets located in neighboring countries. Fortunately, encryption perfectly protects confidentiality and integrity in this case. However, in the context of the current, or future, Gulf crises, availability can only be fully guaranteed if the next generation fiber-optic cable to be connected to Qatar avoids GCC countries altogether and places the nearest socket in India.

Recent Cyber Attacks in Qatar

Like all sovereign states, Qatar is vulnerable to malicious programs that can be classified into several main categories:

Computer Virus: A malicious program that can replicate itself with user assistance, such as by clicking on an email attachment or sharing a USB flash drive;

Computer Worm: A malware program that spreads copies of itself without human interaction and without injecting itself into other programs. Usually, a computer worm spreads by self-replication and carries a payload to delete files or to install backdoors in the operating system in order to later grant access to hackers;

Trojan Horse: A malware program that has a visible useful task, but also includes an invisible malicious action. Trojans are often installed by the host user or the host administrator, either deliberately or accidentally. For example, a Trojan horse can hide in a game program to be downloaded from a website. When active, the Trojan horse can read a confidential document on the user's host, launch a keylogger, or run other malicious tasks;

Ransomware: Malicious programs that threaten a user and ask him to pay a ransom, otherwise the hacker in control of the malware will publish the victim's data or encrypt all his files using a secret key (*crypto-ransomware*). The famous WannaCry ransomware is a worm that infected about 300,000 Windows computers in 2017;

Rootkit: The main purpose of a rootkit is to gain covert privileged access to a machine. The rootkit can install itself by phishing, by password cracking, or by exploiting vulnerability in the system. An attacker may also receive assistance from an insider in the organization to gain administrator access;

Remote Access Trojan (RAT): Malware that allows hackers to remotely control a system via a network connection. One recent example, highly capable of avoiding security scanners, is Kedi, reported in September 2017.

Over the past decade, Qatar has been the target of a dozen major cyber attacks included in one of the above categories. The two most serious events were the 2012 RasGas attack and the 2017 Qatar News Agency (QNA) attack. In August 2012, a virus infection caused the partial blackout of the RasGas computer system in Qatar. RasGas' email servers and website were shut down for many days by the virus, without, according to the company, affecting production operations.

This incident followed an attack on Saudi Aramco, the world's largest oil company, in which tens of thousands of computers were infected by a malware. Indeed, RasGas and Aramco were hit by a modular virus called Shamoon, also referred to as W32.Disttrack. Shamoon is a very aggressive virus with three modules: (1) The first module makes the virus persistent. It also spreads across the local area network by copying itself to other computers. (2) The second module is a wiper capable of overwriting the hard disk. (3) The third module handles communications between the virus and a command-and-control server. Hence, Shamoon is capable of downloading new binary components, remotely changing the disk wiping time, and reporting the damage to the attacker.

In January 2017, Shamoon 2 (W32.Disttrack.B) once more targeted Saudi Arabia, hitting 22 institutions, but no cases were reported in Qatar in this time period. The 2012 Shamoon 1 infection started when an Aramco employee clicked on an attachment in a phishing email. In the case of Shamoon 2, attackers used stolen passwords to make the virus propagate across the targeted organizations.

Experts found evidence that the designers of Shamoon were inspired by followers of the malware Stuxnet: Flame (SkyWiper), Duqu, and Gauss malware. Stuxnet targeted Iran's Natanz nuclear plant in 2010 as part of a cyber strategy by Tehran's opponents to prevent the development of its nuclear program. Flame is considered to be the most sophisticated malware encountered by Kaspersky Lab. However, Shamoon and Stuxnet have infected more computers than Frame.

Shamoon was probably designed by Syrian or Iranian hackers, perhaps supported by a sophisticated third-party state actor. This makes it less likely that Qatar will be the victim of an attack by Shamoon 2 or a newer version in the context of the current GCC crisis. However, a cyber attack based on an updated version of Stuxnet, which expert consensus agrees was designed by the US and Israel in collaboration, is more likely to occur.

The second major cyber attack experienced by Qatar in recent years occurred in May 2017 when hackers took full control of the network belonging to QNA, including accounts with emails and passwords of all employees, websites and social platforms (Twitter and YouTube). Infiltration started in April 2017 and, according to the Qatari Ministry of Interior, the hacker scanned the QNA website using a virtual private network (VPN) to find a vulnerability (the authorities have not revealed its exact type). Three days later, the hacker exploited this vulnerability in order to enter the QNA network and install malware. Over subsequent days, the hacker updated his installed malware and took full control of the main server with access to emails and passwords.

According to the ministry, the hacker twice contacted an IP address in the UAE via Skype to share information. Remote access to the QNA network was also made from remote IP addresses located in neighboring countries. On May 24, at midnight, false reports attributed to Qatar's amir, Sheikh Tamim bin Hamad Al Thani, were uploaded on the QNA website. According to subsequent reports by the Ministry of Interior, the website immediately received unprecedented levels of traffic from the UAE. In less than an hour, the QNA website became unavailable due to this huge surge in traffic. QNA technicians contained the hack at 3am and restored access to the website. The fact that the QNA hacker used a VPN to hide his identity in the infiltration phase, raises the question of why he then contacted an accomplice via Skype with an IP address located in the UAE. A professional hacker could have used a secure way to contact and share information with partners located elsewhere.

One possible explanation is that the hacker used a VPN to directly connect to the QNA network. This is possible if the hacker possessed in advance, by means of theft or provision by a former employee, the credentials of a QNA account holder. Little technical information about this cyber attack, which is widely viewed to have triggered the Gulf crisis, is available. Investigators have not reported the types of malware programs installed by the hacker, nor is the role of the VPN in this cyber attack very clear. The announcement that the hacker stole passwords from the main server also raises issues, given that passwords are stored in their hashed version. One possible assumption is that the hacker installed a keylogger to get clear passwords.

Both the 2012 RasGas and the 2017 QNA cyber attacks severely impacted the fundamental principles of the CIA triad. As noted above, the QNA attack was used as a pretext by members of the anti-Qatar coalition to launch their embargo on Qatar. Apart from these two major attacks, the country has experienced other, more minor, cyber attacks in recent years. For example, in March 2013, Qatar Foundation's Twitter and Facebook accounts were hacked. In October 2013, hackers gained access to the Qatar Domain Registrar managing all domain names ending with ".qa" and modified the DNS records to redirect many important Qatari websites. This was a short-duration attack on availability only. Finally, the data breach at Qatar National Bank (QNB) in 2015-2016 can also be considered as relatively minor. Stealing money was not the hacker's main aim. The infiltration focused on logging transactional data.

The Gulf Crisis and the Cyber Threat

The Gulf crisis, in itself, has no direct influence on the number of cyber incidents or cyber attacks in Qatar. It is possible that a RasGas-type cyber attack could happen in the context of the current hostilities but this would be a major pro-active escalation of a crisis that up to now has taken the form of a diplomatic boycott and economic embargo. Such a move could be categorized as an attack on Qatari infrastructure and would set an unfortunate precedent for regional cyber interactions.

A less grave scenario, along the lines of the QNA hacking, could also occur again as the weakness is in the website software and its maintenance, which allow attackers to remotely compromise a machine or to take control over it.[1] It is possible that such a scenario could occur because of a perennial problem common in every organization: the failure of employees to follow proper security procedures that reduce vulnerabilities. A password can be lost or stolen, and a user can accidentally activate a malicious attachment, as happens across the world a multitude of times daily.

---

1   Other attacks on network security include IP spoofing, IP sniffing, TCP session hijacking, and many DoS attacks based on ICMP and SYN flooding.

Conclusion and Lessons Learned

In order to prepare the country to face future challenges and potential cyber events, Qatar should focus on education and research, on protecting vital systems such as those of its main water and electricity supplier, and on diversifying the location of its fiber optic cables.

Education: Computer programming is fundamental in all tasks related to cyber security. A cyber expert or a cyber technician must also deal with different types of operating systems. Hence, starting from high school and continuing at the university level, students should be taught important programming languages such as C/C++, Java, Perl and Python, and web programming scripts such as HTML, Javascript and PHP.

It is also vital to deepen the understanding of major operating systems including Windows, MacOS, Linux, and mobile operating systems from the kernel up to the graphical user interface. On top of this, a better understanding of the following will also be key: the principles of networking for local networks and the internet; cyber security essentials for students, and continuing education for staff employees and engineers in private and public institutions; and higher levels of mathematic literacy, especially as cryptography, one of the main components of cyber security, requires a strong grounding in mathematics, including number theory and algebra.

Research: In the realm of real-life cyber security, there is little place for theoretical research and the corresponding publications. But engineers and technicians who are members of a cyber team should continue practicing and learning about new systems and new threats. A team may build new software or new systems to detect malware and countermeasure cyber attacks. Such tasks belong to the area of development. Fundamental research is possible in the field of cryptography and other cyber security fields related to cryptography. The research outcome could be used to confirm the validity of practical results found by a cyber team or to suggest new methods to deal with cyber threats.

Cyber security is also very connected to machine learning and to computing in general. Computer clusters can be used to simulate cyber attacks, to do the cryptanalysis of proposed cryptosystems, or to run machine learning software applied to cyber security. Efforts in the computing area should be made in Qatar in parallel to those dedicated to cyber security.

Protecting Vital Sites: Kahramaa was established in 2000 to regulate and maintain the supply of water and electricity for the population of Qatar. It operates as an independent corporation and is the sole transmission and distribution system owner and operation for electricity and water in Qatar. This makes it both extremely important and, what should be considered, the first vital site, on a short-term basis. Indeed, all services require electricity to work, and its absence will paralyze society as a whole. Water is also vital for the needs of the population and the proper functioning and well-being of society as a whole.

Therefore, Kahramaa should prioritize the protection of its industrial control system and its business network. Machines on both networks should be well maintained. Employees should be trained to protect and securely use their credentials. The production sector (companies such as Qatar Petroleum), the communications sector (Ooredoo), and the financial services and banking sector (QNB), are less vital in the short term, as a cyber attack on any one of these areas is less damaging than an attack on Kahramaa.

That said, attacks against targets like Kahramaa are difficult to initiate and only an attack via a sophisticated Flame or Stuxnet-like virus would leave significant damage. Of course, availability could also be threatened in Kahramaa or any other major organization if employee credentials are not well secured or if the main website has vulnerabilities.

We also recommend avoiding the Windows operating system in the top 10% of the most sensitive sites in Qatar.

Fiber-optic Connectivity: Moreover, as noted above in my discussion of the internet backbone (a long-term vital element), the availability of Qatar's access to the internet can be fully guaranteed if, and only if, future fiber-optic cables connect Qatar directly to India. Consequently, very sensitive sites in the State of Qatar should be equipped with satellite communications for emergency situations.

The Gulf Crisis and the Gulf Gas Markets: The Qatari Perspective

STEVEN WRIGHT, HAMAD BIN KHALIFA UNIVERSITY

From a geopolitical perspective, it would not be an understatement to view the Middle East and North Africa as the most complex region globally even for the most experienced observers of international affairs. The region is currently experiencing one of its most challenging periods of upheaval, with relations between states becoming increasingly competitive, erratic and unpredictable. Historically the six Arab Gulf states of the Gulf Cooperation Council (GCC) have been relative havens of security. These six states have proved agile and resilient in the face of major upheaval. Their ability to navigate successive waves of challenges has been enabled primarily by their unique economic model based on their status as crude oil exporters.

Collectively, four of the six GCC states – Saudi Arabia, the UAE, Qatar and Kuwait – are major international exporters of crude oil and have a privileged position in the global energy market as members of the Organization of the Petroleum Exporting Countries (OPEC). Oman and Bahrain do not qualify for OPEC membership because of the smaller size of their oil deposits, but their own more modest exports have still provided the revenues to pay for economic development and have given them the capacity to be politically resilient.

Despite being oil-rich, it is something of a paradox that except for Qatar, these GCC states are all gas-poor, and rely on imports of natural gas to meet their growing domestic needs. It is in this context that the launch of the blockade against Qatar in June 2017 has opened up a new chapter in relations between the Gulf states. This crisis will have many longer-term implications regardless of whether or not a settlement is reached and it raises a number of important questions. In particular, it is essential to consider how this crisis impacts on the role of Qatar as a leading supplier of natural gas, and also how it affects its gas-poor neighboring states in the Gulf who depend on gas imports to meet their domestic needs.

Given their social and cultural links, in addition to the slow yet progressive moves toward regional integration in the economic, political and even security realms, it was reasonable to have concluded that there was a logic to integration based on each state's national interests.[1] Indeed, the move toward increased political and economic integration would have followed other regional models, notably the European Union (EU) and the Association of Southeast Asian Nations (ASEAN). It is in terms of national interests that the role of natural gas has particular importance for the GCC states, given that all members of the GCC, with the exception of Qatar, face shortages of natural gas and have to rely on imports to meet their domestic needs. Natural gas is a strategic commodity that is required for fuel for electricity production, industry and domestic household consumption, in addition to the oil sector where it is used in advanced oil recovery applications. Despite the close linkages that existed within the GCC, in addition to the needs of its neighbors, it is justifiable to ask why Qatar had prioritized the international market rather than its neighboring states for its natural gas exports even prior to the start of this current breakdown in intra-Gulf relations.

The answer to why Qatar's gas policy has been internationally orientated can be explained by the interplay of both commercial and political factors.[2] A fledgling regional gas trade had emerged through the construction of the Dolphin pipeline, which began carrying gas from Qatar to the UAE in 2007, and subsequently Oman in 2008.[3] The initial pricing for the

1   Steffen Hertog, 'The GCC and Arab Economic Integration: A New Paradigm,' *Middle East Policy*, Vol. 14, Issue 1 (2007).

2   James Krane and Steven Wright, *Qatar "Rises above" Its Region: Geopolitics and the Rejection of the GCC Gas Market*, No. 35, Kuwait Programme, London School of Economics, 2014, http://eprints.lse.ac.uk/55336/1/__lse.ac.uk_storage_LIBRARY_Secondary_libfile_shared_repository_Content_Kuwait%20Programme_Krane_2014.pdf

3   Justin Dargin, *The Dolphin Project: The Development of a Gulf Gas Initiative*, Oxford, Oxford Institute for Energy Studies, 2008.

supply of Qatari gas through the pipeline was negotiated in 2002 on an index linked to the price of crude oil, which at that time was at a low point of around $22 per barrel. This proved to be an opportune time for the UAE, and it succeeded in gaining a cheap supply of natural gas. From 2003, the average price of crude oil saw progressive increases in a market cycle of high oil prices which lasted until 2014, and as natural gas is typically priced through a formula linked to the cost of crude oil, any future supplies from Qatar would have been at a much higher rate.

For Qatar, the rising price of crude oil proved to be a golden age for its natural gas sector along with the revenue it received from gas sales. With Qatar's neighbors in the region wanting a discounted rate for natural gas imports, on a purely commercial basis the logic for Qatar has been to embrace the international market. Qatar, therefore, opted to invest heavily in tankers capable of carrying liquefied natural gas (LNG). This gave it a global reach and allowed it to supply gas to the lucrative markets of Japan and South Korea, the Indian subcontinent and Europe. One of the side benefits of Qatar adopting this energy strategy was that it allowed it to develop more substantive political and economic ties with the countries that were purchasing its LNG.

This explains why Qatar decided against providing its GCC neighbors gas at a discounted rate, a move that hindered the emergence of a comprehensive regional gas market. This Qatari decision to premise its energy policy on a firm commercial basis rather than on regional political considerations has proved to be a central reason why the country has been able to fund its rapid economic development.[1] It has also enabled Qatar to engage in a wide-ranging and ambitious foreign policy program that has challenged conventional thinking about the role of small states in international affairs.

As Qatar moved toward an internationally orientated and commercially driven natural gas policy, Oman signed an initial agreement in 2015 to establish a natural gas pipeline from Iran, thereby safeguarding its own future needs. It also served as a pragmatic response to a domestic challenge and underlined Oman's willingness to engage with Iran as an equal partner despite the tensions that exist between Iran and its GCC partners Saudi Arabia and Bahrain. The UAE and Kuwait, along with Saudi Arabia and

---

1   Justin Dargin, 'Qatar's Natural Gas: The Foreign-Policy Driver,' *Middle East Policy*, Vol. 14, Issue 3 (2007).

Bahrain, sourced their natural gas needs from the international market, bypassing Qatar in an explicit demonstration of opposition to its neighbor's determination to sell gas to the highest bidder on a purely commercial basis.

The global and diversified nature of Qatar's energy strategy meant that the current crisis has had no discernible effect on its energy policy. Qatar's LNG tankers have continued to serve its global market unhindered and gas production has been immune from the blockade, thus allowing the country to meet its existing international commitments. Qatar has also continued to supply gas through the Dolphin pipeline to the UAE, despite the severing of relations. From the Qatari perspective, honoring this agreement has served to underline its desire not to exacerbate the situation and to see a peaceful resolution to the crisis. In addition, it also serves to underscore its reputation as a reliable supplier of LNG.

However, while the blockade may not have had any immediate impact, one conclusion that can be reached is that it has closed the door to any future use of gas to drive regional integration. This has longer-term implications for Qatar, as the Gulf market was poised to become an important future market for its gas, given the transformational changes taking place in the global energy system.

The Changing Global Gas Market

Between the early 2000s and 2014, Qatar benefited from being the leading supplier of LNG to global markets in an era of high oil prices. These attractive conditions encouraged innovations in the natural gas sector, in addition to bringing new entrants to the market. This has resulted in a range of transformational changes globally over the last decade, which have significant implications for the way LNG is traded and priced. The principal argument here is that the market has been evolving in response to increased competition, stagnant demand and an oversupply of gas, which have further depressed prices.

The scale of this change is best illustrated by the shale revolution in the United States. The exploitation of shale rock has enabled the United States to emerge as the world's largest producer of shale gas and shale oil. It is also poised to become the largest exporter of natural gas by 2022. It is important to recognize here that with the expansion of the Panama Canal, the transport time for LNG shipments from the United States to the lucrative markets in East Asia has been cut to around 20 days, which enables it to compete favorably against Qatar and other leading international suppliers. Moreover, given its location, it is also in a favorable position to supply LNG to the European market.

The emergence of Australia is also notable. The country has extensive deposits of coal-seam gas, and has also made sizable investments in exploiting this natural resource. It will overtake Qatar as the leading global exporter of natural gas before 2020. This adds to the competitive environment Qatar is having to navigate in terms of its energy policy and underlines the scale of supply coming onto the global market. In 2013, the Russian parliament took a strategic decision to liberalize the energy market to cater for a higher exporting capacity. Since then, Russia has also increased its LNG exports and, by 2020, Russia is expected to have doubled its volume of LNG to half that of what Qatar currently exports. It is also in a strategic position to use pipeline-based supply to the vital Chinese market, which is expected to show growth in gas demand.[1]

Overall, these transformations in the global natural gas sector have resulted in an increase in supply, which translates into a much more competitive market sector, and a potential glut in the gas market. As supply-side competition has grown, there are concerns over future levels of demand for natural gas. Japan and South Korea are collectively the largest international consumers of LNG. Their thirst for gas has made them Qatar's top trading partners in recent years. Yet gas demand in both cases is viewed to have plateaued and it will progressively decline going forward. In the case of Japan, prior to the March 2011 tsunami and the suspension of its nuclear reactors, its energy efficiency measures coupled with a declining population had seen its consumption begin to decline.[2] It was the suspension of all nuclear reactors in the country which boosted the global gas market in an era that was already experiencing oversupply in the market.

For its part, South Korea has embarked on a large-scale expansion of its nuclear power capacity. This will see it reduce its LNG imports over the

---

[1]   Amy Myers Jaffe *et al.*, *China's Energy Hedging Strategy: Less Than Meets the Eye for Russian Gas Pipelines*, The National Bureau of Asian Research, 2015, http://nbr.org/research/activity.aspx?id=530

[2]   Masatsugu Hayashi and Larry Hughes, 'The Policy Responses to the Fukushima Nuclear Accident and their Effect on Japanese Energy Security,' *Energy Policy*, Vol. 59 (2013).

long term. By 2029, it is expected to have 16 new nuclear reactors, seven of which are expected to be completed by 2021.[1] Such moves toward a more diversified energy mix translate into a reduction in LNG imports, which aggravate what is anticipated to be an oversupplied market. With growth projections in Europe also indicating that demand for natural gas has plateaued, the global trend in the gas market is stagnant demand and an oversupply to the market.[2] The only regions where growth in natural gas needs are projected to rise are China, which as mentioned above can capitalize on potential pipeline-based supply from Russia, the Gulf region and the broader Middle East.

For Qatar, these changes in the global natural gas market have heralded a need for a recalibration of its energy policy. Prior to the crisis, Qatar was moving to adapt its energy policy to address these changing realities, and the Gulf gas market, as well as other emerging markets, would have been a natural fit for future sales. Competition from rising producers has meant that a greater emphasis on emerging markets is required to counter the prospect of losing market share. As importing countries look to achieve a diversified supply of natural gas to ensure energy security, other suppliers can benefit at the expense of Qatar and other major suppliers. Additionally, the prospect of an oversupply of natural gas to the global market, coupled with a downward trend in the price of crude oil, translates into a lower return.

This explains why, on the eve of the blockade in April 2017, Qatar lifted its moratorium on the exploitation of its North Field, which is the largest non-associated gas field in the world. Central to this decision was a desire to increase natural gas production, in the hope that rising capacity will help Qatar sustain its global competitiveness, especially in regard to emerging markets. In other words, prior to the current crisis Qatar was already pursuing a pragmatic strategy in the face of global trends in the hope that it would be able to compete and secure market share in emerging markets while maintaining its existing supply relationships.

1   Steven Wright, 'Qatar's LNG: Impact of the Changing East Asian Market,' *Middle East Policy*, Vol. 24, Issue 1 (2017).

2   John Conti *et al.*, *Annual Energy Outlook 2016 – with Projections to 2040*, Washington, D.C., US Energy Information Administration, 2016.

The Gulf Market: A Missed Opportunity

When the above factors are taken into consideration, it is clear that even before the start of the crisis in June 2017, Qatar was poised to shift its energy policy in line with the market environment. In particular, Qatar was uniquely positioned to divert some of its excess supply to meet growing demand in the regional Gulf market albeit at a lower rate. Although Oman pragmatically opted to enter into a supply agreement with Iran to secure its natural gas needs, such a prospect remains an unrealistic proposition for the other GCC states given their political differences with Tehran.

In these terms, the current breakdown in relations among GCC states is a lost opportunity for all states concerned: Qatar's provision of LNG to the Gulf market would have provided it with many benefits, not least that it would have allowed it to secure market share in an emerging market at a time of rising global competition and oversupply. It would also have benefited the consuming GCC states, which would have had a reliable supply of LNG sourced from their own region. Given the scale of the LNG trade, it would also have helped facilitate further economic integration among member states of the bloc. Moreover, given that natural gas could be provided through pipeline-based supply, it also offered the prospect of being more cost effective than having to rely on imports from suppliers such as the United States, which began exporting gas to the UAE and Kuwait in 2016.

Saudi Arabia's current drive to transform its economic model includes the reform of its domestic electricity production, which is heavily dependent on burning its main export commodity of crude oil. A move away from oil-fired to gas-fired power stations would have provided a strategic advantage to the kingdom, while a reliable pipeline-based supply of gas from Qatar would also have provided a mutual benefit to both countries. For Bahrain, which also suffers from a natural gas shortage, meeting its gas needs from Qatar would likewise have proved beneficial for both countries.[1] Moreover, with the Dolphin pipeline in place, the UAE has the potential to achieve energy security by agreeing to higher import volumes from Qatar.

---

1   Ilhan Ozturk and Usama Al-Mulali, 'Natural Gas Consumption and Economic Growth Nexus: Panel Data Analysis for GCC Countries,' *Renewable and Sustainable Energy Review*, Vol. 51 (2015).

Yet the crisis has served to close the door to mutually beneficial trading relationships between the GCC member states.[1]

Conclusion and Lessons Learned

The June 2017 blockade proved to be a pivotal moment in redefining the manner in which Qatar engages both economically and politically in the international system. As this chapter has discussed, transformational changes are underway in the global natural gas market which have clear implications for Qatar and necessitate a reorientation of its energy strategy if it is to maintain its position as the market's leading supplier. It is clear that in the past, Qatar's energy policy was commercially driven, prioritizing contracts with higher paying international partners over local partners seeking a discounted rate. It is also clear that on the eve of the crisis, and in response to increasingly competitive market conditions and potential over-supply, the country was poised to engage more deeply with its regional neighbors in order to establish itself as a secure and reliable supplier of natural gas. That this is unlikely to happen now is a missed opportunity for all the Gulf states and a reminder of the damage the blockade has caused to the national interests of all the parties to the dispute.

---

1   Hisham Khatib, 'Oil and Natural Gas Prospects: Middle East and North Africa,' *Energy Policy*, Vol. 64 (2014).

International Energy Law and the Gulf Crisis

DAMILOLA S. OLAWUYI, HAMAD BIN KHALIFA UNIVERSITY

Between them, the six Gulf Cooperation Council (GCC) member states are some of the world's major exporters of oil and natural gas, and the wider region holds some of the world's largest proven gas and oil reserves. Despite, or perhaps because of, their central standing in the global energy markets, Gulf countries also face common and multifaceted threats to energy security in terms of availability, affordability and accessibility of energy, and the high vulnerability of vital energy systems.

Unprecedented growth in domestic energy demand due to a geometric increase in population and energy consumption, has resulted in a region-wide rise in energy poverty – defined as the inability of households to access electricity and modern energy services at an affordable cost. The sharp fall in oil prices in 2014 has also weakened government earnings, making it difficult for governments across the region to continue and/or complete several ongoing energy expansion projects.[1] There is also a growing realization that oil and gas resources across the Gulf region could be depleted within the next few decades, which has escalated the prioritization of low carbon energy transition and economic diversification. Finally, Gulf countries, as both arid countries and small state actors, face the complex challenge of climate change on energy security in the region, which threatens everything from fatal heat waves to a debilitating rise in sea levels.

Nevertheless, over the last decade, a robust regional governance approach to energy security in the Gulf region, especially amongst GCC

---

1 See Adel Abdel Ghafar, 'Will the GCC be able to adjust to lower oil prices?,' Brookings, 18 February 2016, https://www.brookings.edu/blog/markaz/2016/02/18/will-the-gcc-be-able-to-adjust-to-lower-oil-prices/

countries, has provided a shared and progressive framework for addressing these concerns. For example, in order to address energy poverty in the region, the GCC Interconnection Authority (GCCIA) was established in 2001 to interlink the national power grids of all six GCC countries.[1] Qatar's signing of long-term natural gas supply contracts, most notably with the UAE but also with Egypt, Kuwait and Jordan, had provided an incentive to energy cooperation across the Gulf.

The Gulf crisis casts great doubt on the future of the GCCIA, and could upend future regional cooperation in the vital areas of energy supply and governance. This chapter will examine the domestic and geopolitical implications of the Gulf diplomatic crisis on energy security in Qatar and in the Gulf region. It will then discuss the need for Qatar to develop a robust multilateral cooperative approach, i.e. a two-pronged approach that addresses energy security concerns through increased domestic action, and strategic trade linkages in the global natural gas supply markets, as an important pathway for Qatar to recalibrate and revitalize its energy law and policies in response to the Gulf crisis.

The Gulf Crisis and Energy Security Challenges

While the exact reasons for the Gulf crisis are complex and unclear,[2] its short- and long-term effects on regional energy cooperation and governance are already apparent. This section discusses four challenges thrown up by the Gulf crisis.

Fragmentation and possible end to regional cooperation on energy pricing and supply

One of the most complex threats to global energy security is the deep and growing divide between countries in international treaty negotiations, which has for many years stifled and decelerated international cooperation in addressing energy challenges. For example, the influence and utility of

---

1   Al-Taqrir al-Sanawy, GCC Interconnection Authority, 2009. www.gccia.com.sa/publications/GCCIA_Annual_Report_2009.pdf

2   Bassam Fattouh and Bill Farren-Price, 'Feud between Brothers: The GCC Rift and Implications for Oil and Gas Markets,' Oxford, Oxford Institute for Energy Studies, 2017, pp. 2–3.

the Organization of the Petroleum Exporting Countries (OPEC), as an effective price-modulating oil cartel has waned over the last decade due to divisions, bifurcations and geopolitical alignments. Furthermore, the process of consensus building, especially on the complex issues of oil production quotas, renewable energy development quotas, and energy poverty, has been increasingly complicated.

The Gulf crisis, and the attendant possibility of Qatar developing alignments and positions that could be at variance with other GCC countries, could further complicate global energy cooperation and multilateralism. The GCC has played a major role in deepening international cooperation and multilateralism on energy pricing and supply, by promoting common and coordinated positions for GCC members in multilateral negotiations within OPEC. A recent example is the highly important 2016 agreement reached by OPEC members to limit oil production to 1.2 million barrels per day in response to oil price volatility.[1]

Furthermore, Saudi Arabia and the UAE's central positions and influence in both the GCC and OPEC, raise the possibility of impending structural fragmentation of both organizations, as well as shifting membership policies that could leave Qatar marginalized or excluded. Such an outcome may simply result in Qatar and its allies choosing to pursue a distinctive energy cooperation agenda outside of OPEC, much like that which already exists among several oil and gas exporting giants that are non-OPEC members – such as Canada, Norway, Russia and Australia. Such a scenario, even if it stops short of Qatar's withdrawal or removal from OPEC, may also result in the Doha-headquartered Gas Exporting Countries Forum (GECF) assuming a larger and more significant role in the political economy of energy by morphing into a full-fledged gas cartel. Even if this does not happen, the Gulf crisis could fundamentally weaken or polarize the structural functioning, existence and effectiveness of OPEC, the GCC and the GECF as key institutions in the global oil and gas markets.

Similarly, the Gulf crisis has raised several complex legal questions related to the continuing viability of existing long-term natural gas supply contracts between Qatar and some of the blockading countries. Qatar has

---

1 'Impact of the November 2016 OPEC Agreement on the Oil Market,' *ECB Economic Bulletin*, Issue 8, 2016, https://www.ecb.europa.eu/pub/pdf/other/eb201608_focus01.en.pdf?84e6b1f5356e53c615d6e8e5af195007

taken the commendable decision of continuing to supply gas to the UAE, despite Abu Dhabi's lead role in initiating the crisis. As Qatar's minister of energy has explained: "During this blockade we have never missed a single shipment of oil or gas to any of our consumer partners. That shows how committed Qatar is, not only to our economy and reliability but also to consuming countries."[1]

Nevertheless, any future change of policy direction by Qatar may stifle the availability, affordability and accessibility of energy in the UAE and in the region as a whole. Conversely, a decision by Egypt, the UAE or Jordan to no longer accept Qatari gas, in violation of existing take or pay obligations under supply contracts, may have little or no economic impact on Qatar, given that the majority of Qatar's gas exports go to Asian and European markets. But such a development would have a much bigger impact on the potential utility and profitability of regional pipeline projects such as the Dolphin pipeline.[2]

On the legal level, the crisis has triggered, and could continue to trigger, a wide range of complex litigation and arbitral disputes between Qatar and the blockading countries. The key legal issue at stake is whether, and under what conditions, the parties can be excused in law for not respectively supplying or receiving natural gas in accordance with *force majeure* and/or take or pay provisions under extant long-term natural gas supply contracts. A long drawn-out international dispute on these contractual matters could further exacerbate the Gulf crisis and diminish any remaining appetite for regional cooperation on energy supply and trade.

Threat to integrated regional electricity market in the region

The Gulf crisis may signal the end to an integrated electricity market in the region. Studies have identified a clear need for an interconnected and integrated regional electricity market, as a way of addressing energy poverty

---

1   Anthony Dipaola, 'Qatar says it's fulfilling oil and gas deals despite Gulf crisis,' *Bloomberg*, 13 September 2017.

2   The Dolphin pipeline links Qatar's North Field with markets in the UAE and Oman via a subsea pipeline which supplies around two billion cubic feet of gas a day. See Justin Dargin, 'Qatar's Gas Revolution,' in Bassam Fattouh and Jonathan Stern (eds.), *Natural Gas Markets in the Middle East and North Africa*, Oxford: The Oxford Institute for Energy Studies, 2011, https://www.oxfordenergy.org/shop/natural-gas-markets-in-the-middle-east-and-north-africa

and ensuring security of electricity supply at the most competitive prices in the region. In pursuit of this agenda, the GCCIA was established in 2001 to provide an integrated platform for addressing energy poverty in the region. Furthermore, a Power Exchange and Trade Agreement (PETA) was signed on 7 July 2009, to interlink the national power grids of all six GCC countries.[1] However, since 2009 when the agreement was put in place, electricity trade among GCC countries has remained modest and at a very early stage of development. As the World Bank has argued, achieving a regional electricity market will require an ongoing commitment, as well as political efforts to achieve a harmonized regulatory framework with clear rules governing electricity trade in the region.

The crisis throws into doubt the future of the GCCIA. Furthermore, if the crisis persists, it is unclear whether GCC countries will harmonize their laws and integrate their institutions to sustain and achieve the regional electricity integration goals. Isolating national electricity systems from the integrated GCC-wide energy market could exacerbate energy poverty in the region. Without integrated electricity infrastructure, it would also be difficult for GCC countries to buy and sell electricity at competitive prices across borders. From this perspective, the Gulf crisis raises fundamental questions as to whether, and how, GCC countries can respectively address energy poverty challenges outside of the GCC integrated energy market framework.

Loss of a coordinated approach to addressing the unique impacts of climate change in the region

The Gulf crisis has upended, and could further stifle, a regional-level coordinated approach to addressing the unique threats of, and vulnerabilities to, climate change in the region.[2] Given the dual vulnerabilities of Middle East and North African (MENA) countries to the impacts of dangerous climate change, national authorities in the MENA region have in recent years rightly recognized a clear need for a concerted and collaborative approach to climate change mitigation and adaptation.[3] In addition to developing

1 Al-Taqrir al-Sanawy, GCC Interconnection Authority, 2009.
2 See Damilola Olawuyi, 'Qatar Blockade and Regional Cooperation on Climate Change,' *Climate and Carbon Law Review*, Vol. 11, No. 4 (2017), pp. 330–41.
3 Mari Luomi, 'Bargaining in the Saudi Bazaar: Common Ground for a Post-2012 Climate Agreement?', Helsinki, FIIA Briefing Paper, No. 48, The Finnish Institute of International Affairs, 2009.

proposals for the establishment of a regional ministerial and technical council to provide climate change assessments and possible responses in the Arab system, efforts have also been underway to formulate a clear MENA position at international climate change negotiations to implement the goals and visions of the Paris Agreement, which has been signed and ratified by several MENA countries.[1]

The Gulf crisis directly disrupts continued opportunities for collaborative and collective action on climate change in the region. The need for enhanced regional cooperation in addressing climate change in the MENA region cannot be overemphasized. The Paris Agreement encourages countries to uphold and promote regional cooperation in order to mobilize stronger and more ambitious action on climate change mitigation and adaptation by all parties. Regional interaction and knowledge sharing could help generate greater awareness and political action on climate change in a region that is one of the most vulnerable to the impact of climate change.

Threats to regional efforts on low carbon energy transition

The GCC crisis could upend recent efforts aimed at reducing dependencies on oil and gas revenues and promoting renewable energy in the MENA region. In the immediate pre-blockade era, the development of large-scale renewable energy systems was identified as a national priority in several MENA countries. For example, the Qatar National Vision 2030 (QNV) outlines Qatar's plans to generate 20% of its electricity from solar systems by 2030. Similarly, Kuwait's National Vision 2035, the Bahrain National Vision 2030, the Saudi Arabia National Vision 2030, the Oman National Vision 2020, and the United Arab Emirates National Vision 2021, all contain similarly robust plans for low carbon energy transition. The Gulf crisis, and its resultant impact on regional trade, have placed huge financial and economic stress on the MENA region, and may affect the abilities of MENA countries to finance and achieve their low carbon visions.[2]

Furthermore, the drive to increase government earnings to cushion the

---

1   21 out of 22 Middle East countries have signed the Paris Agreement. See Paris Agreement - Status of Ratification, http://unfccc.int/paris_agreement/items/9444.php.

2   Nader Kabbani, 'High cost of high stakes: Economic implications of the 2017 Gulf crisis,' Brookings, 15 June 2017, https://www.brookings.edu/blog/markaz/2017/06/15/the-high-cost-of-high-stakes-economic-implications-of-the-2017-gulf-crisis.

economic implications of the Gulf crisis may result in more oil and gas production, therefore derailing the low carbon transition plans of GCC countries. For example, in July 2017, Qatar Petroleum announced plans to increase its natural gas production by 20% from its North Field. It is estimated that this move will raise Qatar's total liquefied natural gas production capacity by 30% to 100 million tons per year. This represents the lifting of a decade-long self-imposed moratorium on North Field production.[1]

The decision to do this, at the height of the Gulf crisis, has signaled Qatar's drive to solidify its domestic economy and maintain its position as the world's largest exporter of liquefied natural gas. However, the renewed focus on natural gas production in Qatar may slow down progress in achieving another vital goal by 2030 – "a diversified economy that gradually reduces dependence on hydrocarbon industries."[2] Furthermore, if the regional crisis persists, other Gulf countries may rapidly expand their own oil and natural gas production, and plans were already underway prior to the blockade to boost natural gas production in Saudi Arabia.[3] If this results in an increase in natural gas production in the region it could retard the progressive plans to phase out hydrocarbon dependence, and associated GHG emissions, in the region.

Advancing Energy Security in Qatar: Opportunities

The Gulf crisis has cast uncertainty on the future of regional cooperation on energy security and governance. However, the crisis also provides opportunities for Qatar to clarify, recalibrate and consolidate its domestic commitment to energy security and governance through a robust multilateral cooperative approach, i.e. a two-pronged approach that addresses energy security concerns through increased domestic action and through strategic trade linkages in the global natural gas supply markets.

First, the crisis provides an opportunity for Qatar to achieve greater

---

1   See 'Qatar announces huge rise in gas production amid diplomatic crisis,' CNBC, 4 July 2017.

2   *Qatar National Vision 2030*, Government of Qatar, General Secretariat for Development Planning, 2008;
    Qatar National Development Strategy 2011–2016, General Secretariat for Development Planning, 2011.

3   'Saudi Arabia to increase natural gas production,' *Middle East Business Review*, 8 June 2016.

self-sufficiency in energy pricing and policy. The blockade has triggered, and may continue to result in, a range of amendments or reforms to some of Qatar's long-term energy supply contracts, and regional gas supply and pricing policies, to achieve a distinctive energy regime for the country based on its national interests. The ensuing policy reform process provides a chance for Qatar to emerge from the crisis with a strong domestic position, without any regional constraints, that allows it to re-strategize its gas supply and trading arrangements. For example, the crisis might result in the scaling up of Qatar's strategic gas supply arrangements in European and Asian markets, while revisiting gas pricing concessions that could have been made regionally prior to the Gulf crisis.

The crisis also provides opportunities for Qatar to infuse its existing domestic climate change and energy security agenda with greater ambition and focus. Over the last decade, Qatar has demonstrated regional leadership on climate change issues.[1] Apart from hosting the international climate change negotiations in 2012, and taking a lead in signing and ratifying the Paris Agreement, Qatar has also established a national climate change committee as a focal point on climate change issues. The country can now go further and revitalize its climate change agenda by scaling up domestic investment in climate-smart infrastructure – including buildings, structures and systems that reduce GHG emissions, and improve the country's ability to adapt to, and cope with, the risks posed by climate change. Furthermore, the current situation also provides an opportunity to boost investment in renewable energy projects that achieve its low carbon transition agenda and boost electricity supply from alternative and cleaner sources.

Additionally, the Gulf crisis provides opportunities for Qatar to leverage its comparative advantage as the world's largest exporter of liquefied natural gas, to assume greater leadership roles in international energy diplomacy. Any disruption in the production, supply and pricing of Qatar's natural gas could affect its reputation in the global gas market, which could compel European and Asian markets to turn to Russian gas, which is a much less attractive political option for many existing importers of Qatari gas. To neutralize the possibility of this happening, Qatar must look to consolidate its leadership and reputation in the gas market. To do so, it could invest

---

1   Damilola Olawuyi, 'Qatar regional leader in addressing climate change,' *The Peninsula Qatar*, 26 November 2017.

greater effort in developing external global multilateral and bilateral cooperative relationships and strategic gas supply linkages that focus less on regional geopolitics.

Conclusion and Lessons Learned

This chapter addressed the domestic and geopolitical implications of the Gulf Crisis on energy security in Qatar and the Gulf region. It also examined whether a multilateral cooperative approach to energy governance may provide a robust pathway for Qatar to recalibrate and revitalize its energy law and policies in response to the Gulf crisis. Several of the energy security challenges facing the Gulf region are interconnected and cannot be addressed in isolation. International energy law therefore emphasizes the continued importance of, and need for, political cooperation to advance regional, as well as global, energy security. The implications of the Gulf crisis for energy security in Qatar can be mitigated through increased domestic action, and the scaling up of strategic trade linkages in global natural gas supply markets. Greater emphasis should also be placed on pursuing an energy policy and agenda that avoids competitive and conflictive geopolitics, but instead focuses on fully leveraging Qatar's comparative advantage in the natural gas market, to assume greater leadership roles in international energy negotiations and governance.

The Other Gulf Cold War: GCC Rivalries in Africa

HARRY VERHOEVEN, GEORGETOWN UNIVERSITY IN QATAR

Following the imposition of the embargo on Qatar in June 2017 by Saudi Arabia, the United Arab Emirates (UAE), Egypt and Bahrain, the political struggle between the Gulf states quickly moved from the Arabian Peninsula to the other side of the Red Sea. In the weeks that followed, Riyadh and Abu Dhabi frantically drummed up support in Africa for their isolation of Doha in an attempt at demonstrating broad agreement with their gambit in international society. Persuaded by undisclosed monetary incentives, Chad, Comoros, Mauritania and Senegal cut diplomatic relations with Qatar altogether while Djibouti, Gabon and Niger downgraded them. Further rhetorical support was offered by a Saudi-Emirati proxy in Libya, General Khalifa Hafter of the Libyan National Army and the unrecognized Tobruk government, who virulently denounced Qatar's "support for extremism and terrorism." Leaders of various federal entities in Somalia also broke ranks with the government in Mogadishu's official stance of neutrality and sided with Abu Dhabi and Riyadh, as did the breakaway republic of Somaliland. However, the two most important target states of the Bahrain-Egypt-UAE-Saudi coalition, Eritrea and Sudan, elected to balance their praise for the coalition's efforts to combat terrorism with statements reiterating their respect for Qatar. Ethiopia, the dominant regional power in the Horn of Africa, too decided not to pick sides, thereby implicitly backing Doha.

This chapter will first situate the diplomatic waves caused by the 2017 Qatar crisis in a broader trajectory of relationships between the Gulf and Africa, which has recently acquired much greater economic importance to the Arabian Peninsula. These economic determinants are complemented by intensifying political rivalries among member states of the Gulf Cooperation Council (GCC) themselves and with Iran: what can be termed the "other Gulf cold war." This chapter will then explore the political, security and economic motives for the intensification of the involvement of Qatar, Saudi Arabia and the Emirates in Africa in recent years and show that this engagement is structural and not merely short term and transactional. Both the long-term prosperity of key Gulf states and their security is increasingly seen as contingent on developments on the continent – particularly in the Horn of Africa. Finally, the chapter will highlight some of the repercussions of both these underlying trends and the recent Gulf spat and formulate some conclusions as to how the Qatar-Africa relationship could be rendered more symbiotic.

Africa and the Gulf: an Old Relationship Deepens

The societies of Africa and the Gulf have long been connected and for centuries have profoundly moulded each other in the fields of commerce, culture and politics. The development of the three great monotheistic religions is testament to these interactions, as are the spread of Arabic and culinary, musical and sartorial exchanges. Yet not all interaction has been positive: the legacy of the Indian Ocean and Red Sea slave trade still casts a long shadow over Arab-African relations and, together with experiences of contemporary racism, continues to generate distrust and animosity on the continent vis-à-vis Gulf societies.

The glitzy rise of the Gulf in the last 45 years upended the relative symmetry in power relations that historically prevailed between Gulf Arabs and Africans. While GCC states have gained global influence and accumulated vast wealth, African states have struggled to guarantee their citizens basic socio-economic and political rights and have become net recipients of Gulf overseas development assistance. For the first decades after 1973 and the oil price hikes, the economic relationship was mostly defined by humanitarian aid to charitable and religious causes from Senegal to Somalia – notwithstanding some notable exceptions, like Sudan, where strongly politicized investment objectives were pursued.

In the last 10 to 15 years or so, the economic significance of Africa to Gulf states has been transformed. The most eye-catching factor has undoubtedly been the dramatic spike in commodity prices. When in 2007-2008 Asian states banned rice exports and grain prices spiralled out of control, food riots erupted in several North and Southern African countries and fears of a Malthusian crunch returned to the Arabian Peninsula. The prospect of running out of food and water compelled sovereign wealth funds and holding companies from Qatar, Saudi Arabia and the UAE to aggressively move on international markets with a view to buying up or leasing productive land and concluding long-term agreements to secure uninterrupted supplies. Soaring prices have made the cultivation of previously marginal land attractive; the geographic proximity of East Africa, with all its cultural similarities, represents an obvious pull factor for Gulf investment into agricultural projects.

Concerns about food and water security have been flanked as determinants of Gulf activity by more apparently commercial motives. Arab companies have seized important positions in the telecoms, banking and hospitality sectors as well as opening for-profit schools, launching mining operations and acquiring valuable real estate – and Gulf-owned enterprises have been central to these moves. Improved macroeconomic management in many African states and reduced exchange rate volatility and inflation are helping to attract foreign capital. The 2010 report by management consultancy firm McKinsey, "Lions on the Move," has embodied this newfound gusto about African markets. Reports of an emerging middle class, with greater than hitherto appreciated purchasing power, have underpinned bullishness about economies like Ethiopia's and Kenya's: the claim is that the return on foreign direct investment in Africa is higher than anywhere else in the developing world and that the continent's urbanization will yield a permanent consumer bloc that could revolutionize demand for foreign and African-made goods.

"Consumer-facing" industries, infrastructure and agriculture across the continent could generate more than $2 trillion in revenue annually, which would turn the likes of Ethiopia, Kenya and Sudan into African equivalents of Asian Tigers. Beguilingly, McKinsey has been important not just in altering perceptions regarding Africa's investment climate, but also in drafting reforms in the Gulf as well, notably in partnership with the office of Saudi Crown Prince Mohammed bin Salman. It is widely understood that Riyadh's vaunted Saudi Vision 2030, which aims to reduce the kingdom's oil dependence and diversify its economic base, was strongly inspired by the management consultancy giant. This economic rolling of the dice by Mohammed bin Salman matters greatly for Africa. Even if investments into Asia and Europe remain the priority, capturing a small fraction of the $2.5 trillion available to Saudi Arabia to implement Vision 2030 would result in a bonanza for any African state.

This trend in Doha, Riyadh and Abu Dhabi of looking toward Africa to recycle petrodollars has been strengthened by the hundreds of thousands of Sudanese, Somali, Eritrean and Ethiopian professionals working on the Peninsula. Many of these have been conduits for advice and channelling capital inflows from Gulf economies into their countries of origin. Moreover, diaspora returnees to Africa in the last decade have brought substantial savings with them from North America, Europe and the Gulf, which has boosted domestic demand and expanded the banking and services sector. Combined with years of sustained economic growth, itself driven by high commodity prices and expanding cities, this has bolstered the disposable income of a small but meaningful middle class in Addis Ababa, Khartoum and Nairobi. There is now a constituency – perhaps 20-25 million strong across the Horn of Africa – that has enough purchasing power to acquire some of the consumer goods that multinational corporations provide. Whereas 30 years ago the number of potential customers for any major investor was too limited to warrant the complex procedures required to establish operations on the continent, today's growing market size is changing the cost-benefit ratio as evinced by the inflow of capital from Kuwaiti telecom operators, Qatari property developers and Saudi banks.

Growing Securitization of Gulf Involvement

The surging importance of Africa to Gulf food and water security as well as to long-term commercial diversification has been supplemented in the last decade by an increasing securitization of the relationship – as evident both before and since the outbreak of the 2017 Gulf crisis. This is a function of the growing economic interdependence, but also the product of two geopolitical fault-lines.

Firstly, the standoff between Iran and Saudi Arabia is the master cleavage that shapes much of the violence and diplomatic jockeying in the contemporary Middle East. This security dynamic has increasingly been extended to Africa. Tehran believes that the Saudi-American alliance is the root cause of regional dysfunctionality, economic stagnation and political impotence. In the Iranian view, only armed resistance can roll back the trident of US imperialism, Zionist aggression and Wahhabism; hence the importance of the nuclear program and its extensive support for anti-Israeli and anti-American proxies across the wider region, from Beirut to Sana'a. Riyadh, for its part, is convinced that Iran seeks to undermine the stability of the Gulf and encircle Saudi Arabia with Shia (or at least pro-Iranian) regimes in Bahrain, Iraq, Syria and Yemen. King Salman and Mohammed bin Salman are supported in this strategic assessment by Emirati Crown Prince Mohammed bin Zayed who, like his Saudi peers, believes that Tehran is still pursuing the same revolutionary foreign policy that it launched in 1979 when the Islamic Revolution led by Ayatollah Khomeini toppled the long-ruling, pro-Western Shah.

Africa's eastern flank is an extension of the battlefield of the Saudi-Iranian rivalry, with Tehran and Riyadh accusing each other of seeking to use African allies to commit aggression against the other. Because the Al Saud dynasty sees Iran as an existential threat, no efforts are spared to counter it. This has meant rallying all GCC states to support the Saudi-led war in Yemen. It has also required persuading Eritrea, Sudan and Somalia, through investments, loans and central bank to central bank transfers, to ally with the pro-Saudi camp and to keep the Iranian navy out of the Red Sea. Khartoum's decision to cut off ties with Tehran in 2016, despite a previously close politico-military relationship which allowed Iranian vessels to use Port Sudan, should be seen in light of this. Both Sudan and Eritrea have sent ground troops to participate in the Yemen war and the Eritrean port of Assab is crucial to Saudi and Emirati airstrikes on Houthi targets.

The second geopolitical fault-line stimulating an intensified interest in Africa is enmity between Gulf states themselves – a cold war with its own set of proxy conflicts that sometimes turn violent. While Saudi Arabia continues to see itself as the unassailable regional hegemon to which all others must play second fiddle, Qatar and the UAE feel both capable of and entitled to an independent foreign policy in which they pursue their own interests and promote their own ideological visions for the Middle East, North Africa and the Horn of Africa. They cannot match the sheer size of the Saudi armed forces, but, by virtue of their oil and gas wealth and nimble financial management, Doha and Abu Dhabi possess material resources that

put them in the same league as Riyadh. Emirati and Qatari aid and investment into the Horn is often driven by the same geopolitical objectives as
that of their Saudi friends-cum-rivals: commercial projects are first and
foremost meant to consolidate political relations and gain greater influence
in regional politics; any profit they might yield is a welcome bonus but not
an expected outcome of many of these undertakings.

Qatar has sought to project influence on the continent since the early
2000s through spectacular real estate developments, hundreds of millions
of dollars invested in archaeology, culture and heritage projects (particularly in Sudan) and the extensive operations of Qatar Charity, which is
widely lauded by on-the-ground partners for its effectiveness. Since 2008-
2009, it has sought to bring peace to Darfur by acting as the mediator
between the Sudanese government and Darfurian rebels, and it played a
prominent role in the ousting of Colonel Muammar Qaddafi of Libya and
Hosni Mubarak of Egypt during the 2011 Arab Spring. The latter two
involvements, which included a central role for the Al Jazeera Arabic news
network especially, triggered bitter resistance from Saudi Arabia and UAE.
Both have sought to roll back the rise of the Muslim Brotherhood and other
Islamist groups and to return Libya and Egypt to authoritarian rule under
General Khalifa Haftar and General Abdel Fattah Al Sisi respectively.
Billions of dollars and, in the case of Libya, direct Emirati military intervention, have been committed by Riyadh and Abu Dhabi to counter what is
perceived to be unwarranted Qatari meddling. The deployment of Saudi
and Emirati fighter jets to Assab and the announcement of an Emirati military base in Berbera (Somaliland) further underscore the extent to which
the Gulf cold war (with Iran and among Gulf states) is leading to the securitization of African shores.

The African Perspective

How then are these cold wars between Saudi Arabia and Iran and among
Gulf States perceived in Africa? Until recently, surging Gulf attention –
whether by Qatar, Saudi Arabia, the UAE or Iran – was usually received
positively: the ability to attract greater aid, investment and trade flows,
without having to deal with a normative political agenda (as in the case of
Western engagement) or with the risk of labor immigration and job loss (as
in the case of China), offered incumbent governments the prospect of

strengthening their grip on power and the ability to balance Western and Asian suitors. Yet the progressive securitization of the relationship with the Gulf and the growing demands of Gulf states that African states align politically and confront certain domestic players, most notably Islamists, are swelling concerns. Since the early summer of 2017, some of the indirect consequences patently illustrate the explosive potential of Gulf antagonisms for Africa.

As mentioned above, the Saudi-Emirati initiative led to a bidding war for the loyalties of Africans, with Riyadh and Abu Dhabi seeking to persuade states to rupture diplomatic ties with Qatar. One of the countries that downgraded its relations with Doha was Djibouti, notwithstanding the fact that approximately 450 soldiers of the Qatar Armed Forces have since 2011 been patrolling the Djibouti-Eritrea border following a conflict between those countries. Faced with this major expression of distrust and with the need to bolster its defenses at home, Qatar decided to withdraw its troops, leading to an immediate Eritrean occupation of contested strategic positions along the border. The United Nations and other international partners have since been worried about a flare-up of the conflict, not least because of the influx of Saudi and Emirati cash into the Asmara of President Issayas Afewerki, to reward Eritrea's pivotal contribution to the war in Yemen. This has shifted the balance of power in the Horn of Africa and emboldened Eritrea vis-à-vis Djibouti and its nemesis, Ethiopia. The latter fears Issayas will use the money to destabilize the region in general and Ethiopia's fragile ethno-political compact in particular. Hawks in the ruling party in Addis have been advocating renewed military pressure on Eritrea – a strategy that risks reigniting the 1998-2000 Ethio-Eritrean War that claimed the lives of more than 100,000 people.

The Gulf crisis has also exposed cracks in the federal project in Somalia, with different Gulf actors supporting rival leaders at different levels of government. At the urging of the Western-led international community and neighboring Ethiopia, Somalia's political elite adopted federalism in 2012 as a form of power sharing among various clans and in order to overcome the problem of the concentration of authority in Mogadishu that had turned the regime of Siyad Barre (1969-1991) into an increasingly vicious autocracy. While a politically cogent response that allows for the balancing of different interests and the representation of peripheral areas and previously excluded minorities, the very fact that such state reform could only be achieved because thousands of foreign troops protected the nascent institutions against the jihadists of Al-Shabab highlighted the fragility of the construction. Put differently, in the absence of a strong domestic political consensus and a concentration of coercive power, a united international community is a necessary condition to ensure that Somalia's federal government and its regional states can gradually build up the institutions required to govern the country after decades of civil war; about half of the puny government budget ($267 million in 2017) is paid for by external partners.

In the last five years, however, the increased use by Ethiopia, Qatar, Saudi Arabia, Turkey and the UAE of proxy forces in Somalia – including political parties, security services, presidential candidates and regional governments – steadily sapped the cooperative spirit required for successful state building and nation building. The Gulf crisis has only exacerbated this: after newly elected President Mohamed Abdullahi "Farmajo" Mohamed declined Saudi and Emirati cash in exchange for ending diplomatic relations with Qatar, Abu Dhabi and Riyadh provided millions of dollars to the heads of the regional states of Puntland, Galmudug and Hirshabelle to pressure and undermine the president. Their defiance of Farmajo and bypassing of federal structures in order to strike their own deals with Saudi Arabia and the UAE highlight not only how feeble a federal Somalia remains. Worryingly, it also threatens greater instability. The institutional crisis in Somalia has coincided with an upsurge in attacks by Al-Shabab, including the 14 October atrocity when more than 400 civilians were murdered in Mogadishu: the truth remains that if it were not for foreign troops and money, the jihadists would once again overrun the federal republic.

Conclusion and Lessons Learned

This chapter has underlined how the Gulf has grown into a major actor on the African scene, and, conversely, how Africa has become increasingly vital for Gulf security and long-term prosperity. This new standing has led to the securitization of the Horn of Africa in particular by Saudi Arabia and the UAE; the continent is identified as a key site to secure loyalties, through threatening and cajoling with hard cash, as amply displayed after the imposition of the embargo on Qatar in 2017. The Gulf and Africa are deeply connected because of structural factors, with important implications for bilateral and multilateral diplomacy.

In terms of the current Gulf crisis, it was no coincidence that three of Qatar's long-standing partners – Eritrea, Somalia and Sudan – all resisted strong pressure from Riyadh and Abu Dhabi and refused to rupture diplomatic ties. They also made it clear that Doha will retain the important role it has recently played in their respective foreign policies. Ethiopia, which historically has distrusted Qatar but recently improved relations, also opted for neutrality. This points to the crucial importance of building and maintaining long-term relationships in Africa that endure, even at times of geopolitical turbulence or economic recession. As a small state that is heavily dependent on foreign trade and foreign labor, Qatar needs partners in its near abroad who stand by external partners who demonstrate long-term commitment to the continent in its struggle to tackle poverty, infrastructural weakness and international marginalization.

Apart from increasing the magnitude of its engagement with Africa, this also means that Qatar should invest in the quality of that commitment. African states have often been taken advantage of and foreign investment on the continent has a long (and for the most part) infamous track record, underpaying Africans for their resources and strengthening narrow elites in power who reproduce the very state weakness that other states fret about in security terms. Aid, investment and trade deals that propound broad-based opportunities for much wider sections of society and that do not displace communities have rarely been part of the Gulf's historically elite-centred approach to Africa. The Gulf crisis offers an opening to change that and for Qatar to seize the moment and lead Gulf-Africa relationships into a new era of more balanced, inclusive and sustainable partnerships.

Section 3:
The Crisis in the Media

Twitter as an Instrument of Foreign Policy: Qatar and the GCC

BANU AKDENIZLI, NORTHWESTERN UNIVERSITY IN QATAR

Since the launch of the anti-Qatar blockade in early June 2017, the four Gulf Cooperation Council (GCC) countries involved in the conflict – Qatar, Saudi Arabia, the United Arab Emirates (UAE) and Bahrain – have found themselves in a diplomatic conflict that is being fought aggressively on social as well as traditional media. US President Donald Trump, arguably the world's most powerful Twitter user, set the tone. On 6 June 2017, one day after the blockade of Qatar began, he tweeted: "During my recent trip to the Middle East I stated that there can no longer be funding of Radical Ideology. Leaders pointed to Qatar – look!" The same day, he followed up with a subsequent tweet that made the nascent crisis even more visible on the international stage.

Online, the hashtag translating as "cutting ties with Qatar" became the number one trend worldwide with more than one million mentions at the time of writing.[1] A short-term suspension of Al Jazeera Arabic's Twitter account also underscores how much of the commentary, rumors and back-lash surrounding this crisis has taken place online. The UAE was the first blockading country to ban demonstrations of sympathy toward Qatar on social media, making such actions punishable with a jail term of up to 15 years and a fine of at least 500,000 Dirham ($136,000). Bahrain followed soon after, with the Information Affairs Ministry in Manama issuing a statement on 8 June 2017 that declared any expression of sympathy with the govern-ment of Qatar or opposition to the measures – whether through social media,

---

[1] 'Social media react to Gulf diplomatic rift,' *Al Jazeera*, 5 June 2017.

Twitter, or any other form of communication – a criminal offence punishable by up to five years in prison and a fine. A day later, Qatar's communication office, in what can interpreted as a retaliatory move, urged citizens and residents to take the high road and to mind "Islamic and Arab values" on social media for the duration of hostilities.

The ways that citizens and residents of the region voiced their opinions on social media reveal some interesting patterns. The first is a new sense of nationalism: Many users have relied on songs and cartoons to express support for their respective leaders. The drawing of Qatar's Amir, Tamim bin Hamad Al Thani, by Qatari artist Ahmed bin Majid Almaadheed, became an avatar for many on social media accounts. The attempt to dispel rumors is also of note: The hack of Qatar News Agency (QNA) and the fabrication of statements attributed to Sheikh Tamim on Iran, Hamas and Israel during the last week of May 2017, were published on Qatari news sites and social media. Despite the fact that Qatar was quick to respond and publicize the hack, this incident was soon after used as a pretext for the blockade. Since then users have been quick to point out fake Twitter accounts that spread fake/false news and to warn against propaganda; "#don't participate in suspicious looking hashtags," a hashtag that began trending in August 2017, is a typical example of this.

Another development of interest is the increase in stories of hardship: In addition to severing diplomatic ties and closing their borders, blockading countries also recalled their citizens from Qatar and ordered Qataris to leave their countries. This resulted in the separation of many families during the holy month of Ramadan. Discussions of this on Twitter were understandably emotive. Some examples included tweets drawing attention to "unforgettable, unforgivable moments of the blockade"; tweets expressing discontent over "expulsion from Brother countries, places" (Mecca and Medina, most notably) during Ramadan and "having to wait for Saudi's permission to perform Umrah or Hajj"; and tweets about a "son not being able to attend a father's funeral."

Humor has also been an important part of the online discourse on the crisis. Political satire and humor can often help people deal with political crises and even serve to alleviate anxiety. This can be seen regularly in the context of this crisis. A now famous moment came when the editor-in-chief of the Saudi newspaper *Okaz*, Jamil Al-Ziabi, commented on Al Arabiya TV that Qatar would eventually be forced to accept the demands of the coalition ranged against it on the grounds that "Qatar's stomach will not be able to get used to Turkish and Iranian products."[1] Social media users were quick to respond by posting funny memes and tweets, and the Arabic hashtag translating to #Qataristomach quickly became a trending topic.

This chapter will focus on how Twitter was used during the first 100 days of the GCC crisis as an instrument of foreign policy. Governments tweet daily, and the ways in which a sovereign state represents itself online can offer insights into patterns of representation of state identity, strategy, emotional expression and recognition of others. This chapter will concentrate specifically on English-language tweets by the ministries of foreign affairs of Qatar and the three blockading GCC countries – Saudi Arabia, the UAE and Bahrain. English-only tweets are the focus, in order to examine how regional leaders chose, during this 100-day period, to communicate and present themselves to their targeted foreign audiences, as well as to their own English-speaking audiences at home.

The data for this research is taken from a study conducted by this author during a fellowship at the University of Southern California's Center for Public Diplomacy.[2] This chapter examines eight Twitter accounts: (1) the official personal accounts of the four respective GCC ministers of foreign affairs embroiled in the crisis, and (2) each of the four country's official ministry of foreign affairs accounts. Table 1 presents the accounts.

Table 1. List of Twitter Accounts

Country	Qatar	Bahrain	UAE	Saudi Arabia
Accounts	@ MBA_AlThani__	@Khalidalkhalifa	@AbZayed	@AdelAljubeir
	@MofaQatar_EN	@bahdiplomatic	@MOFAUAE	@KSAMOFA

A total of 1,517 tweets were analyzed for this chapter (110 English tweets from the ministers themselves and 1,407 tweets from the accounts of the

---

1   'Twitter explodes with funny memes after #Qataristomach goes viral,' *The Peninsula Qatar*, 12 June 2017.

2   Banu Akdenizli, 'Digital Diplomacy in the Gulf: An Analysis of Embassies, Foreign Ministries and Foreign Affairs Ministers' Twitter Accounts,' University of Southern California, Center for Public Diplomacy, https://uscpublicdiplomacy. org/research_project/digital-diplomacy-gulf-analysis-embassies-foreign-ministries-and-foreign-affairs

four respective ministries of foreign affairs). Data for this study was collected with the help of the Qatar Computing Research Institute's (QCRI) Social Computing Department.

Table 2. Follower and Following (Friends) Numbers for GCC Foreign Ministers

Foreign Minister	June 2017	September 2017
UAE	3,948,153 followers // 620 friends	4,093,859 followers // 632 friends
Saudi Arabia	1,432,427 followers // 57 friends	1,874,633 followers // 57 friends
Bahrain	382,384 followers // 668 friends	434,604 followers // 668 friends
Qatar	60,929 followers // 29 friends	181,429 followers // 29 friends

Table 2 and Table 3 note the number of followers and the number of accounts followed (friended) by the ministers and the ministries during the period under examination. All accounts increased their follower numbers during the period under study, with Qatar's minister seeing the highest percentage rise, almost tripling the number of followers between June and September 2017.

Table 3. Follower and Following (Friends) Numbers for GCC Ministries of Foreign Affairs

Ministry of Foreign Affairs	June 2017	September 2017
Saudi Arabia	1,146,233 followers // 94 friends	1,401,080 followers // 165 friends
UAE	411,185 followers // 160 friends	442, 014 // 163 friends
Qatar	25,653 followers // 43 friends	39,111 // 51 friends
Bahrain	53,047 followers // 32 friends	56,483 // 31 friends

Social media provides an environment where political entities can interact with their target audience easily. To follow other accounts is, to a certain degree, a way to demonstrate how symmetrical and dialogical the communication of ministers and the ministries is. It may not be possible to follow back all followers but it should be considered important to follow back influencers, accounts that produce effective or informative content or the target audience accounts, especially in times of crises. This has the advantage of providing information on stakeholders, and offering monitoring of online discussions, crises and opportunities. The numerical imbalance between the follower and friends for all the accounts examined in this study signals that ministers and ministries are not making full use of this function.

Who Tweeted the Most and How Often? The Ministers

The Twitter activity of the four relevant foreign ministers varied widely. The Twitter participation of these senior officials is evident from the number of tweets made during the period under study. Despite having the lowest follower and following numbers, the foreign minister of Qatar was the most active during the first 100 days of the blockade. He was responsible for almost half of the sample of English-language tweets of the four ministers (49.5%). The UAE's minister was second (30.5%), followed by Bahrain's top foreign policy decision-maker (20%). Interestingly, the Saudi minister did not tweet in English during the first 100 days of the blockade. As far as the foreign ministries themselves are concerned, almost half the tweets belonged to the Qatari ministry (43%). Bahrain (29%) and UAE (22%) came in second and third. The Saudi ministry only tweeted 85 times during this entire period, less than 1% of all the tweets made during the 100 days under study.

Ministers were sporadic in their tweeting activity, not tweeting at all on some days, tweeting repeatedly on others. On 17 August, for example, Qatar's foreign minister tweeted four times end to end. He expressed his condolences for the Barcelona terror attacks, then tweeted about his meeting with Sweden's moderate party leader, and subsequently about his meetings with his Swedish and Norwegian counterparts. On 1 July, the UAE's foreign minister also tweeted four times in quick succession. His first tweet dealt with a report that Iran had recruited over 10,000 Afghan refugees to fight "battles in Syria," another was a link to a *Los Angeles Times* article on childhood obesity, and a third was a TED talk by famed chess champion Gary Kasparov on intelligent machines. On 29 August, the Bahraini foreign minister tweeted four times, one after another: twice on North Korea firing a missile over Japan (@khalidalkhalifa: "Today's missile fired by N. Korea is a serious unprecedented threat to the safety and integrity of Japan to world security & stability"). The other two were on more random matters – a retweet by a Bahraini citizen, probably a teacher,

warning others not to steal their students' work, and a tweet in which the
minister praised artificial intelligence (@khalidalkhalifa: "The new big
thing is #ARkit"|).

What Did the Ministers Say about the Blockade?

Of all the tweets by the four ministers, 40% dealt with blockade; 35.2% did
not address any specific issue or story in particular; and 9.5% covered official visits and meetings (informing followers about engagements with local
or foreign dignitaries either at home or abroad, usually accompanied by a
photograph). Yet when all the tweets on the blockade are examined, a clear
content creator emerged. Qatar's foreign minister was responsible for 83.3%
of the total tweets on the crisis, his Bahraini counterpart followed with
9.5% and the foreign minister of the UAE came third with 7.1%.

Apart from differences in the frequency and quantity of tweets, the
content of the tweets dealing with the blockade is also notable. Qatar's
foreign minister focused extensively on matters related to international
dialogue and diplomacy efforts ("deep and positive discussion today with
members of @UKHouseofLords on #GCC crisis. #Qatar remains a strong
& trusted partner in the region," dated 6 July; "positive discussion today in
#Berlin w/my friend FM @sigmargabriel. We both agree that the unjusti-
fied blockade on #Qatar is unacceptable," dated 9 June).

Bahrain's foreign minister was more direct: Two examples being – "In
one sentence I heard the word 'blockade' & 'air routes are open over Iran &
through Kuwait, Muscat and Turkey'! Make up your mind Qatar," dated 20
June; "Thank God we are immensely more rich with wonderful creative
people than material wealth, and more thankful for not being nouveau
riche," dated 6 August. The UAE minister did not tweet at all himself in
English on the subject of the blockade in its first 100 days; instead he
retweeted Donald Trump's infamous early tweets on Qatar and the
blockade.

While 85% of the Qatari foreign minister's tweets focused on the crisis
and international diplomacy, the foreign ministers of Bahrain and the UAE
engaged with other topics, some of them lighthearted. "R.I.P Glen Campbell,
Country legend, who gave us a lot more than Rhinestone Cowboy, that will
keep him alive forever," was a tweet from the Bahraini minister dated 8
August; he also wished followers "Happy Social Media day! It made our

lives more exciting," dated 30 June. The UAE foreign minister shared articles from across the international media on a variety of topics including education, healthcare, art and science (for example, on the Salzburg Festival, on 19 August; and on artificially-intelligent painters from the *New Scientist*, on 21 August).

This clear difference of content production and dissemination among the three ministers who engaged in English tweets in this time period demonstrates that at least when it came to English content, Qatar's minister used Twitter as a tool to broadcast more content, recognize others, and share information specifically on the blockade and foreign affairs. In these terms, Qatar's Foreign Minister, Mohammed bin Abdulrahman Al Thani, used Twitter as a more strategic tool of communication in comparison to his Bahraini and Emirati colleagues during the first 100 days of the crisis.

What Did the Ministries of Foreign Affairs Have to Say?

A somewhat different picture emerges when one examines the Twitter activity of the four ministries of foreign affairs over the first 100 days of the blockade. These government institutions tweeted more in terms of volume and frequency than their top officials did from their own accounts. The Qatari ministry of foreign affairs was the most active of the four overall with 43.6% of all coded tweets in this time period. Bahrain (29.4%), the UAE (21.55%) and Saudi Arabia (5.5%) followed. The Qatari ministry account was also the only one of the four accounts to tweet at least once a day and it reached, on occasion, up to 27 tweets in a single day. On 14 June, the ministry not only tweeted about the blockade, it also shared back-to-back infographics on the "types of human rights violations resulting from cutting diplomatic ties #Qatar." These included breaches in freedom of the press, expression and opinion, movement, education, residency and private property; these tweets were accompanied by others reporting on the day-to-day business of the minister: "#Ugandan President Meets Minister of State of Foreign Affairs" or "Foreign Minister @MBA_AlThani_Meets #Turkish Counterpart."

Retweeting and replying to others are common practice on Twitter. Retweeting or passing along a tweet from another feed allows, in theory, an

individual to forward another user's tweet to their own audience.[1] None of
the four ministers or their ministries engaged in much retweeting during
the first 100 days of the crisis – one-third of all tweets by the foreign ministers were retweets (30.5%) and the number for the ministries was even
lower at 24.1%.

The reply tweet is a special type of Twitter activity representing an
exchange share between one account and another specified Twitter user in
a public fashion. The practice of "talking" to one's audience can be regarded
as an act of trying to build a relationship and develop transparency of interactions. During the first 100 days of the crisis, there were almost no examples
of the ministries in question or their ministers interacting with their audiences in this way. In fact, there were only two instances (23 June and 6
August) that a ministry (on both occasions the Bahraini one) replied to a
public individual.

In terms of "big stories" – news stories that are covered in multiple news
outlets for more than one news cycle – the ministries were all preoccupied
almost evenly with two ongoing events: the blockade (33.5%) and the
Visits/Meetings category (33.2%). The ministries were addressing the
regional diplomatic crisis at the same time as they were presenting a "business as usual" face to their followers. The Qatari and Bahraini ministries
were responsible for the largest number of blockade-related tweets (44.6%
and 39.9% respectively), followed by the UAE (10%) and Saudi Arabia
(5.5%).

Like their ministers, the four ministries also differed in how they tweeted
about the blockade. The Qatari foreign ministry made frequent use of infographics in its feeds, highlighting the extensive international reaction to the
blockade, live tweeting Foreign Minister Mohammed bin Abdulrahman Al
Thani's 9 June interview on the BBC, his Al Jazeera TV interview on 12
June and his Royal Institute of International Affairs (Chatham House)
speech in London on 5 July. This demonstrates a clear strategy to supple-
ment traditional media coverage with online resources and was distinguished
by regular references to "dialogue as a strategic choice."

The English tweets from this account rarely used hashtags pertaining

---

1   'How Mainstream Media Outlets Use Twitter,' Pew Research Center Journalism
     Project, 14 November 2011, http://www.journalism.org/2011/11/14/how-main-
     stream-media-outlets-use-twitter/

directly to the blockade – #GCC crisis and #QatarBlockade were used fewer than three times in the period under study. That said, 86.5% of all tweets contained a geographic marker hashtag, marking the tweet with a country and/or city name. Hashtags enhance visibility, since they can potentially be read by individuals who are not following a specific account. Here the prolific use of hashtags indicates a clear understanding of methods to enhance visibility. In the case of Qatar, in particular, its ministry's tweets would almost always contain #Qatar and then an additional country hashtag.

The Bahraini ministry's tendency to send back-to-back tweets distinguishes it from the other ministries examined in this study. On 5 July, the account offered 23 tweets one after another detailing the press conference between the foreign ministers of Saudi Arabia, the UAE and Egypt. This was followed up two days later, with 24 tweets on 7 July after the publication of a joint statement by the four main members of the anti-Qatar coalition (Bahrain, Saudi Arabia, the UAE and Egypt) in response to Qatar's negative response to their list of demands for an end to the crisis.

The Bahraini ministry also regularly highlighted Egypt's vital role in supporting the security and stability of the Gulf region, stressing and affirming brotherly relations with the Sisi government and the people of Egypt. The UAE and Bahrain also focused on the theme of terrorism in tweeting about the blockade. A tweet from the Bahraini foreign ministry of 7 July stated that Qatar's rejection of coalition demands reflected its links to terrorism. On 10 August, the UAE foreign ministry's Twitter account commented on the presence of Taliban members in Doha, which they described as a hub for extremists.

As noted above, the Saudi ministry of foreign affairs rarely tweeted in English in this period, but on the few occasions that it did the focus was also on Qatar's connections to terrorism: "Demands on #Qatar to stop funding terrorism are non-negotiable," dated 1 July. Saudi Arabia was the only country during the 100 days that used its Twitter feed to reference Iran: "#Iran sponsors terrorism and fuels sectarianism," dated 16 June and "#Iran's activities in the region are very negative and has to stop in order to have genuine dialogue with them," dated 20 July.

Conclusion and Lessons Learned

Social media tools, as mentioned earlier, can afford a mutual transmission process between political entities and their publics. If the use of Twitter in foreign policy is about developing relationships, fostering horizontal communication, eliciting feedback, listening and not declaring, then it is safe to say that none of the four GCC foreign ministers at the center of the crisis made great use of the medium during the first 100 days of the blockade. They mainly used the tool to reach their audience and disseminate their message. The extensive use of hashtags, infographics, photographs and links embedded in tweets demonstrate that all four countries, in particular Qatar, have a good understanding of the inner-workings of the medium.

The data underscores that Twitter is mainly used in the Gulf region to broadcast and to draw attention to speeches and announcements; to make and respond to statements; and to present oneself, acknowledge and recognize others and build allegiances. The data also shows that the digital diplomacy of the first 100 days of the blockade, on Twitter at least, mirrored official diplomacy strategy, and was used to make public matters more visible and, at the same time, to help spread the dominant societal actor's discourse.

Research consistently shows the rapid rise in the use of social media across the region[1] among an increasingly connected and engaged public. Regional leaders are well aware of the potential of social media to craft an image online, and to communicate messages between GCC countries and across the entire world. They are also keen to portray themselves as tech-savvy, forward-thinking, modern leaders.[2] Yet it remains to be seen if the blockade will provide the context and platform for the evolution of digital interaction and online dialogue between key regional foreign policy actors or whether it will remain a forum for one-way broadcasting and the dissemination of messages.

---

1   E. Everette Dennis, Justin D. Martin and Rob Wood, *Media Use in the Middle East 2017*, Northwestern University in Qatar, 2017, http://mideastmedia.org/survey/2017/

2   Banu Akdenizli, 'A Snapshot of How Foreign Ministers in the Gulf Use Twitter,' University of Southern California, Center on Public Diplomacy, 2 May 2017, https://uscpublicdiplomacy.org/blog/snapshot-how-foreign-ministers-gulf-use-twitter

The Editorialization of "Hard News" Reports in the Gulf Crisis:

A CASE STUDY IN THE POLITICS OF TRANSLATION

ASHRAF FATTAH, HAMAD BIN KHALIFA UNIVERSITY

In the onslaught of media coverage that has accompanied the Gulf crisis, the line between hard news and opinion has often been blurred. Journalists writing hard news reports on the blockade of Qatar have employed various rhetorical strategies to turn ostensibly objective news into editorialized reports masquerading as facts. This chapter will focus on the ways that authors of Arabic trans-edited news reports in an Emirati newspaper rely heavily on "attribution," i.e. directly or indirectly quoting statements, views or value-laden assessments from outside sources, as a form of editorialization by the back door. I will use the term trans-edited as a general term to describe the processes of translation and adaptation involved in news production. Use of these sources seeks to enhance credibility and legitimize the political position of both the author and the newspaper. It will be argued that the patterns of attribution, as well as ideologically motivated translation shifts, ultimately reveal the attitudinal orientation of journalists who attempt to influence their readers toward the political position of the newspapers they write for.

The focus here will be on hard news reports, which are supposed to deal with news rather than views, hence the claims of objectivity or neutrality often made, somewhat complacently, by the media organizations in question. The present study belongs to a growing body of literature on the rhetorical and ideological potential of hard news reports, attempting as it does to reveal the various overt and covert manifestations of their ideological and attitudinal potential, which lurks behind a veneer or pretension of objectivity. In particular, the study focuses on a selection of putatively hard news reports from the news sections of Abu Dhabi's state-owned *Al-Ittihad* newspaper.

Theoretical Considerations

The theoretical model adopted here for analyzing attributed evaluations in hard news reports is based on the appraisal framework developed by Martin and White.[1] This provides a useful means of identifying the evaluative use of language – the linguistic choices made by speakers or writers that reveal their true feelings, attitudes or stances on a particular matter.

The appraisal framework encompasses the various mechanisms or devices expressing writers' or speakers' attitudes and evaluative positioning. This approach to critical discourse analysis covers three semantic domains: attitude, which is concerned with feelings; engagement, which is preoccupied with the resources by which the authorial voice positions itself with respect to other voices and positions in the discourse; and graduation, which addresses grading attitudes, adjusting the strength of feelings or the sharpness of boundaries between different categories.

The domain of attitudinal assessments is further divided into three semantic subtypes: affect, judgment and appreciation, concerned respectively with emotions, ethics and normative assessments of human behavior and aesthetics and other systems of social valuation. All subtypes of evaluation can be positive or negative, explicit (inscribed) or implicit (invoked). Explicit evaluations (inscriptions) are stable regardless of their context (e.g. disgusting, honorable or ugly), while implicit evaluations (tokens) are activated through contextually dependent inferences and associations.

Another major distinction made in the appraisal framework, especially significant in our present case study of hard news reports, is related to the source of evaluation – whether it is the author (authorial) or a quoted external source (attributed). While attribution is generally perceived by journalists to be compatible with neutrality, it is they who decide to select a particular quote or quoted source. Significantly, this act of selection

---

1   James R. Martin and Peter R. White, *The Language of Evaluation: Appraisal in English*, New York: Palgrave Macmillan, 2005.

signals an author's stance on the attributed material, as well as his or her attempt to influence the reader on a specific issue. Equally significant, from the evaluative standpoint, are ideologically motivated shifts in the translation of attributed propositions or viewpoints.

The Case Study Data

The news reports analyzed in this case study were selected from a special section devoted to the Gulf crisis in the UAE's Arabic daily *Al-Ittihad.* The government-controlled press in the UAE, one of the three GCC members of the anti-Qatar coalition, has taken a progressively negative stance toward Qatar since the outbreak of the crisis in the summer of 2017. The crisis manifested itself with escalating media hostilities in the wake of US President Donald Trump's visit to Saudi Arabia on 20 May 2017. This expressed itself in the form of the reported hacking of Qatar News Agency (QNA) on 24 May and the attribution of remarks critical of US foreign policy to the Amir of Qatar, Sheikh Tamim bin Hamad Al Thani.

This crescendo of media hostility was particularly evident in *Al-Ittihad,* which from 29 May onwards allocated a two- to four-page section to political, economic and sport news about Qatar, first called "The Hijacked Qatar" and then "Qatar Commits Suicide," explicitly attitudinal titles for a section that was essentially supposed to be a hard news section and that was immediately followed by the views section. This special section, almost exclusively comprised of negative news reports about Qatar, was discontinued on 13 October 2017. The current study confines itself to news reports published in this section of *Al-Ittihad* newspaper over the month of September 2017, with particular emphasis on reports involving explicit attribution to outside sources, i.e. trans-editing attributed material into Arabic.

Before turning to the discussion and analysis of the selected news reports, a few words need to be said about the typical structural and evaluative features of hard news reports. This term is used here to refer to common factual reports recounting news events (such as accidents, natural disasters, violence, conflicts, wars, etc.) rather than articles explicitly providing the journalist's opinions or views, hence the common claim of objectivity and impartiality often associated with hard news reports.

Typical examples would be the news wires produced by news agencies and articles published in the news sections of newspapers or on the websites of news organizations. Hard news reports typically have an inverted pyramid structure, with the headline and lead of the report encapsulating the maximally newsworthy elements of the story and the body reiterating, contextualizing and elaborating on those elements.

Another characteristic feature of hard news reports is the pattern of evaluative meanings they exhibit, which is termed "reporter voice" to denote the fact that they are generally devoid of explicit expressions of authorial affect or judgment of human behavior.[1] Arguably, the textual architecture and evaluative profile of the wires produced by such international news agencies as Reuters, the Associated Press (AP) and Agence France-Presse (AFP) are generally maintained in their Arabic language versions, on which hard news reports published by Arabic media outlets tend to be modelled. For the purpose of this paper, the term "editorialization" of hard news reports is used in the very general sense of an overall tendency to use those reports as a vehicle for expressing views rather than reporting news.

Discussion and Analysis

Analysis of this case study data reveals distinct strategies employed by the journalists in question to editorialize hard news reports while largely retaining their architectural structure, thereby giving them a semblance of objectivity. One of the most striking features of editorialization in the news reports analyzed is the inclusion in the hard news section of explicitly evaluative graphics and images demonizing Qatar or its government, for example, by portraying it in the form of a snake, crow, pirate-ship or even a washing machine for money laundering. Another common feature is the frequent use of so-called "kickers" – extra headlines set in a smaller point size above the main headlines, where the journalists, among other things, provide editorializing comments about the story in question. To take one example, a story whose main headline was "African Websites: Egypt Reveals to Chad Qatar's Conspiracies" carried the kicker "Among the Series of Scandals Doha is Implicated In."

Since this study is focused on the evaluative workings of trans-edited

---

1   Peter R. White, 'Media power and the rhetorical potential of the "hard news" report–attitudinal mechanisms in journalistic discourse,' *Käännösteoria, ammattikielet ja monikielisyys. VAKKI: n julkaisut*, Vol. 36 (2009), pp. 30–49.

attributions, the following analysis will be largely devoted to attitudinally significant translation shifts in instances of attribution to external voices, whereby hard news reports come to function as disguised editorials with seemingly credible, though conveniently distorted, attributions intended to position or persuade the reader to take a negative view of Qatar.

As a general rule, almost all the trans-edited observations, views and assertions directly or indirectly attributed to external sources in the news reports in question involve explicit or implicit negative attitudinal assessments of Qatar, which cannot necessarily be said of the original attributions. Frequently, the attribution to a particular source is carefully managed so that negative assessment is selected to the exclusion of any potentially positive assessment of Qatar or negative assessment of the blockading countries provided by the same source in the same report.

An example that epitomizes this pattern of managed attributions is a news report about Iran's role in the crisis,[1] in which the *Al-Ittihad* journalist quotes an editorial article written by Mohamed Ayoob[2] for the *National Interest* online magazine.[3] According to the *Al-Ittihad* version, Ayoob asserted that "it is Iran which is moving Qatar in its feud with Arab countries in order to win a new battle in what he [Ayoob] called the 'cold war' between it [Iran] and Saudi Arabia in the Middle East." But in the original editorial, Ayoob simply made the argument that Iran had won another round in the "Saudi-Iran cold war" thanks to Saudi Arabia's "own folly" and "miscalculations" in the Gulf crisis.

Thus, the trans-edited attributed material is evaluatively distorted to posit, and shift the reader toward, a different rhetorical position, where Iran is scheming to prod Qatar into rejecting the demands of the blockading countries. The journalist uses such reporting verbs as "(the report) reveals" and "(the report) demonstrates," which show the journalist's sympathy toward these twisted attributions. This mode of attribution is intended to cast both Iran and Qatar in a negative light by dint of such carefully selected negative tokens as "it is Iran which moves"; "Qatar's

---

1 'Iran Leads Qatar in in Escalating Crisis,' *Al Ittihad*, 7 September 2017.

2 Mohammed Ayoob is professor emeritus of International Relations, Michigan State University, and senior fellow, Center for Global Policy.

3 Mohammed Ayoob, 'The Saudi-Qatar crisis amounts to a big win for Iran,' *The National Interest*, 4 September 2017.

enmity/feud with Arab countries"; and "Qatar's rejection of the demands of anti-terror countries."

In addition to using negatively distorted selections clearly meant to align readers against Qatar, the *Al-Ittihad* journalist deselects from the source article any positive tokens about Qatar (and Iran) or, more importantly, negative tokens about Saudi Arabia. Notable among these are the following sentences and phrases contained in Ayoob's original piece:

- This outcome is largely the result of Saudi Arabia's own folly
- Riyadh forced Qatar into a diplomatic corner believing that Doha, in response to the quarantine imposed upon it by Saudi Arabia and its Gulf allies, will come running back to big brother hat in hand
- Qatar forcefully rejected all Saudi demands
- Second, Saudi Arabia failed to take into account the value attached by Washington to America-Qatar relations
- Despite President Trump's anti-Qatar remarks, uttered in total ignorance of Qatar's strategic value to the United States
- Protected by these two factors, Qatar could thumb its nose at the Saudis
- Qatar has now done exactly that with gusto
- Saudi Arabia's ill-considered moves against Qatar has also contributed to the rapprochement between Ankara and Tehran
- Saudi Arabia, as a result of its miscalculations – based more on hubris than anything else – has paved the way for the latest Iranian diplomatic victories

Had these value-laden elements been selected by the *Al-Ittihad* journalist, the article would have conveyed the opposite attitudinal stance. Another strategy frequently deployed by the journalist to add legitimacy and credibility to the negative stance adopted toward Qatar is the blurring of distinctions between the authorial and attributed voices through integrated attribution (reported speech). Thus, a reader confronted by the following integrated attribution would assume that the positively evaluative qualification "the countries calling for fighting terrorism" was actually used by the quoted external expert, thereby legitimating the negative authorial stance toward Qatar: "The report demonstrates that Iran is seeking to encourage

Qatar to reject the demands of the countries calling for fighting terrorism (Saudi Arabia, UAE, Bahrain and Egypt)."

The same could be said of the ostensibly attributed phrase "Qatar's feud with the Arab countries," which implies that the quoted external expert is of the view that Qatar's position is antagonistic to that of the entire Arab world. Readers of the Arabic report are subliminally driven to make this assumption, unless they are consciously engaged in a critical discourse analysis of the kind undertaken here.

Another example that clearly demonstrates how the selection, source and mode of attribution are managed in trans-editing to align readers into an attitudinal position opposed to Qatar is a report with the self-congratulatory headline: "Bloomberg Highlights *Al-Ittihad*'s Reports about Qatar's Attempts to Undermine the Cooperation Council."[1] This article involves explicit attribution to the Bloomberg news agency, with a hint of positive evaluation by Bloomberg of *Al-Ittihad*'s reports, and hence the credibility of those reports, thanks to the token "highlights." In other words, *Al-Ittihad*'s reports about Qatar's purported attempts to undermine the GCC are so credible as to be worthy of being foregrounded by Bloomberg, which, as the source of attribution, is prominently designated in *Al-Ittihad*'s article as the "international agency" and the "well-known agency" to enhance the credibility and legitimacy of *Al-Ittihad*'s reporting. The body of the report confirms this initial perception with further evidence of twisted and blurred attribution, which is evaluatively loaded:

> The international agency Bloomberg has highlighted reports published by *Al-Ittihad* [newspaper] about the efforts to undermine the GCC, in the light of consistent indications coming from Qatar and its allies about the Doha government's desire to leave the Council, on the pretext that it lacks any role and on account of its alleged "failure" to provide protection for the "isolated emirate" in the midst of the crisis which has resulted from its subversive and foolish policies.

Note the nested attribution and carefully selected attribution devices employed in this convoluted lead of the report: *A highlighted that B reported*

---

1   'Bloomberg highlights *Al-Ittihad*'s reports on Qatar's attempts to undermine Co-operation Council,' *Al-Ittihad*, 1 September 2017.

that C indicated/alleged, i.e. *A appreciates the truthfulness of B; B is telling the truth; C is lying*. It is hard in this attribution to distinguish the voice responsible for the explicit negative judgment ("isolated," "subversive," "foolish"), which is yet another clear manifestation of editorialization of ostensibly hard news reports. The reader would be forgiven for ascribing the explicitly negative judgment to the "well-known" and "international" news agency that has "highlighted" *Al-Ittihad*'s reports. The following is another passage from the *Al-Ittihad* article centered around Bloomberg:

> Bloomberg shed light on *Al-Ittihad*'s assertion, quoting from a research paper written by an expert in Gulf affairs in a unit affiliated with Al-Ahram's Centre for Strategic and Political Studies, that "Doha's rulers constitute a threat to the Gulf countries' security and stability." The well-known agency also highlighted the title "Qatar commits suicide" chosen by *Al-Ittihad* for its daily section covering developments in the Qatari crisis.

Here, we note the same pattern of nested attribution and the dignified status of the attribution sources: "an expert in Gulf affairs"; "the well-known agency." In addition, the "highlighting" of a clearly loaded title for hard news reports about the Gulf crisis, without any evaluative comment by Bloomberg, is astonishing. If we turn to Bloomberg's English-language source report,[1] we readily observe how its author's value position is distorted in trans-editing. Indeed, if anything, the Bloomberg reporter seems to be negatively disposed to the position of the blockading countries, as indicated by the following evaluative tokens, which are conspicuously, albeit understandably, absent from *Al-Ittihad*'s report: "UAE media jump on Qatar"; "chatter that Qatar wants to quit the GCC"; "In pages upon pages of copy … they accused the gas-rich emirate of plotting to serve Iran"; "'Qatar's treason'" and "'Qatar commits suicide,' the newspapers screamed"; and "Abu Dhabi's state-owned Alittihad proclaimed."

Commenting on reports in UAE newspapers that Qatar sought to leave the GCC, the Bloomberg reporter makes the following two propositions without any explicit conjunction (see Table 1):

---

1   Zeinab Fattah, 'U.A.E. media jump on Qatar over report it plans to bolt GCC,' *Bloomberg*, 30 August 2017.

i. Qatari officials have never publicly expressed any intention to leave the GCC.

ii. An editorial in a privately owned Qatari newspaper echoed the sentiment of many in Qatar who are angry with the GCC.

Table 1

Bloomberg's Report	*Al-Ittihad's Trans-edited Report (Backtranslation)*
Qatari officials have never publicly indicated any intention to leave the bloc, and officials have repeatedly invoked mediation as the way to resolve the conflict within the GCC. An editorial Tuesday in Qatar's privately owned Al Arab newspaper echoed the sentiment of many in Qatar who are angry at the GCC for not supporting them against the Saudi-led bloc's actions. Leaving the council "has become a popular demand because Qatar will stick to its position that rejects guardianship," the editorial said.	In what seemed to be a reference by the international agency Bloomberg to the contradiction between public statements issued by official circles in Qatar and what is broadcast by media outlets known to be close to the authorities there, the agency [Bloomberg] said that Qatari officials have never publically indicated any desire to leave the GCC, but it [Bloomberg] referred at the same time to an editorial appearing in the Qatari Al Arab newspaper on Tuesday in which the newspaper claimed that many in Qatar feel angry at the GCC for allegedly letting their country down in the current crisis. Indeed, [it also noted] how this editorial went as far as claiming that leaving the GCC 'has become a popular demand'.

Given the various attitudinal clues in the article, the overall rhetorical position of the author suggests that the implicit conjunctive relation between (i) and (ii) above is one of concession in the sense that Qatari officials never expressed their intention to leave the GCC in spite of popular anger with, and a demand for leaving, the organization. However, through twisted attribution, *Al-Ittihad*'s reporter[1] conveys a negative assessment of Qatar on the part of the Bloomberg reporter; this is achieved through the following mechanisms of manipulation involving evaluative trans-editing shifts:

1. Falsely attributing to Bloomberg a perception of contradiction between the two propositions (i) and (ii) above by inserting an interpretive comment adjunct ("In what seems to be a reference to contradiction …") and the concessive conjunction *but* ("the agency [Bloomberg] said that … but it [Bloomberg] referred at the same time to an editorial …").

2. Ascribing to Bloomberg distancing modes of attribution thereby

---

1   'Serious repercussions for Qatar's "reckless" actions,' *Al-Ittihad*, 1 September 2017.

casting doubt on the veracity of media reports which suggest popular anger in Qatar with the GCC ("claimed" and "allegedly")

3. Legitimating the perception of contradiction by falsely attributing to Bloomberg the observation that those press statements have been issued by media outlets "known to be close to the [Qatari] authorities," and thus should be taken with a grain of salt or interpreted as emanating from official circles, hence the contradiction.

4. Other rhetorically motivated shifts include, for example, "conflict within the GCC" rendered as "current crisis"; "Qatar's privately owned Al Arab newspaper" rendered as "the Qatari Al Arab newspaper"; "Leaving the council 'has become a popular demand…' the editorial said" rendered as "Indeed, [Bloomberg also noted that] this editorial went as far as claiming that that leaving the GCC 'has become a popular demand'"; conveniently omitting the reason for Qatar's position: "because Qatar will stick to its position that rejects guardianship."

This pattern of politically motivated shifts and distortions in translated attributions is prevalent in the news reports examined here. It frequently manifests itself as sensationalist headlines with shifts in the source and mode of attribution: "Merkel: Qatar has Violated Human Rights to Build World Cup Stadiums," whereas Merkel's original statement was that Amnesty International had accused the emirate of numerous human rights violations. Thus, the accusation becomes a statement attributed to an authoritative source, namely the German chancellor, and situated in the headline as the maximally newsworthy element of the report.

Another gross distortion of attribution can be found in the headline: "Qatar Foreign Minister: The 'Brotherhood' is Terrorist and We Support It." This attributed statement is a mistranslation of a statement made by Qatari Foreign Minister Sheikh Mohammed bin Abdulrahman Al Thani during an interview[1] with the Fox Business Network, in which he said: "So, regarding Al-Qaeda, Muslim Brotherhood and all the terrorist org… and any terrorist organization, Qatar is not supporting."

---

1   'Qatar does not support terrorism: Qatari foreign minister says,' *Fox Business News*, 18 September 2017.

Conclusion and Lessons Learned

The above discursive analysis of a selection of news reports published in the news section of *Al-Ittihad* newspaper about the Gulf crisis has revealed the ways journalists have adopted attribution strategies aimed at casting Qatar in a negative light in the current crisis, while presenting a façade of detachment and neutrality typical of standard hard news reports. Thus, the ideological and evaluative orientation of the journalist is hidden behind a cover of hard news reporting, in which trans-edited attributions of outside sources are often evaluatively twisted or distorted. This back-door editorialization of hard news reports, relying as it does on ideologically motivated shifts in the translation of attributed material, seeks to enhance credibility and achieve legitimation of the authors' and the newspaper's political position. In a sense, the journalist is piggybacking on external, authoritative sources to align the reader into a false universal position that is negatively disposed toward Qatar.

This analysis has also demonstrated that attributed observations, values and views are carefully selected and reworked to advance an explicit or implicit negative assessment of Qatar to the exclusion of any potentially positive tokens or even any negative assessment of the blockading countries. Ideologically motivated selections and transformations by means of translation shifts and manipulations are heavily deployed in hard news reports to achieve political ends. Hiding behind the liberal selection of lengthy negative quotes, the authorial voice of the news reports seems to negatively evaluate Qatar by proxy. They also position the reader to adopt an equally negative view. Thus, this study highlights the inherently subjective and evaluative nature of hard news reports, as well as their potential to be employed as a political tool, in crises such as the current one in the Arab Gulf.

How International Media Tackled the Blockade

CHRISTINA PASCHYN, NORTHWESTERN
UNIVERSITY IN QATAR

Since the start of the Gulf diplomatic imbroglio in June 2017, international media coverage has varied depending on the news publication's readership and the national interests of the country in which the outlet is based. This chapter will explore how media coverage in the editorial pages of conservative and liberal publications differed, with a specific focus on opinion pieces published digitally by *The Telegraph* and *The Guardian* in the United Kingdom and Fox News and CNN in the United States.

UK Publications

In the years immediately prior to the blockade, the British media was largely critical of Qatar. Both the conservative *Telegraph* and the liberal *Guardian* had published editorial pieces lambasting the country for its poor migrant rights record and had voiced opposition to Qatar hosting the 2022 World Cup. Where both publications differ, however, is in their attitudes toward Qatar following the imposition of the blockade.

The author analyzed editorials published between the blockade's launch in June 2017 and February 2018, using the word "Qatar" as the search term. During this period, 19 opinion pieces in the *Telegraph* discussed Qatar in the context of the crisis. About seven expressed a generally negative attitude toward the country, viewing the diplomatic row as something that Qatar had brought upon itself due to its alleged support and financing of Islamist groups in the region, implying support for the blockading countries' stance against Qatar, or denouncing Qatar in some way.

Seven pieces maintained a somewhat neutral tone. Some mentioned Qatar and its position under the blockade only briefly as part of a larger story on a particular topic (such as the airline or football industries). Other pieces that covered the blockade with more depth refrained from making strong value judgments on the veracity of the accusations against the country, or they drew attention to the failings of the boycotting countries, as well as Qatar, in terror financing and in other problematic areas.

An example of this form of neutral coverage includes the *Telegraph* View of 5 June, in which the blockading countries are accused of imposing "draconian measures" on Qatar, while acknowledging that the allegations that Qatar supports radical groups are "not entirely without foundation."[1]

Coverage that can be construed as sympathetic or more positive toward Qatar number five in total. These include a 5 July opinion piece by Yousef Ali Al-Khater, the Qatari ambassador to the United Kingdom, which strongly rejected the accusations of the blockading countries and expressed the hope that the Gulf nations would be able to "resolve our differences as brothers."[2] Editorials that used sympathetic terms that characterized Qatar as facing an "impossible" situation and/or demands, are also examples of positive coverage.[3]

The most passionately argued pieces on the *Telegraph* site are largely negative in tone. For instance, from mid-June to November, the *Telegraph*'s Defence Editor Con Coughlin published four editorials expressing disdain for Qatar, from its sponsorship of Britain's Royal Ascot and "decades of ridicule and political meddling" in other Gulf nations,[4] to its alleged support of Islamist groups.[5] In September and October 2017, two of his op-eds expressed a pro-Saudi stance. His 26 September piece titled, "We won't

---

1   Telegraph View, 'Terror will be the winner if Gulf states and Qatar don't mend their fences,' *The Telegraph*, 5 June 2017.

2   Yousef Ali Al-Khater, 'Qatar's crisis can only end if we sit down together and resolve it as brothers,' *The* Telegraph, 5 July 2017.

3   Jeremy Warner, 'UK's ambivalent attitude to Qatar threatens to scupper Aramco IPO,' *The Telegraph*, 26 August, 2017; Anthony Harwood, 'Qatar's friends in the Gulf are driving it into the "fangs of wolves",' *The Telegraph*, 3 July 2017.

4   Con Coughlin, 'Britain can't avoid being dragged into the brewing Qatar-Arab Cold War,' *The Telegraph*, 14 June 2017.

5   Con Coughlin, 'By fixating on Brexit, Britain risks a further erosion of its influence over global affairs,' *The Telegraph*, 21 November 2017.

beat terror by turning our backs on Saudi Arabia and Egypt," criticized the British decision to sell warplanes to Qatar. "By signing the deal, though," he wrote, "we seem to be conveniently overlooking Qatar's well-documented role in financing and supporting Islamic extremists..." He also warned that the "deal also risks alienating Saudi Arabia, a vital intelligence-sharing partner in the fight against Islamic extremism."[1]

Coughlin's piece on 24 October titled, "Britain must remember who its real friends are in the crisis engulfing the Middle East – and they don't include Qatar," also described Saudi Arabia as a close ally of Britain. He praised the country for its modernization efforts tied to its Vision 2030, which he says may prove financially beneficial for the United Kingdom, and praised US President Donald Trump for cultivating a closer relationship with ruling elites in Riyadh and for taking a "stand against state-sponsored terrorism." The same praise, he argued, could not be lavished on the British government, which he once again reminded readers was willing to sell warplanes to Qatar.[2]

The *Guardian*, on the other hand, seems to have taken a more sympathetic view of Qatar's plight following the launch of the blockade. Of the 10 editorials that comment directly on the crisis, about six are more positive in tone toward the country and four can be described as relatively neutral. For instance, in a 7 June piece that primarily attacked US President Trump and questioned his competency in dealing with the Gulf crisis, the *Guardian* editorial board did not shy away from criticizing Qatar, stating that it is "no liberal democracy: it's an absolute monarchy with an appalling record on labour rights." Overall, however, the piece can be read as expressing support for Qatar. It called the demands of blockading countries for Qatar to close the Al Jazeera news network "absurd." In discussing Qatar's Islamist connections, it made the important point that the Qatari government has hosted the Taliban and Hamas "with the tacit approval of the US, which wants such groups isolated but around to talk to." The piece also contrasted the foreign and domestic policy visions of Qatar and Saudi Arabia in a way that

---

1   Con Coughlin, 'We won't beat terror by turning our backs on Saudi Arabia and Egypt,' *The Telegraph* 26 September, 2017.

2   Con Coughlin, 'Britain must remember who its real friends are in the crisis engulfing the Middle East – and they don't include Qatar,' *The Telegraph*, 24 October 2017.

tacitly endorses the former's political autonomy and its somewhat more progressive religious-cultural development:

> The root of today's troubles can be traced back to 1995, when the current Qatari ruler's father ousted his pro-Saudi father from power. Saudi Arabia and the UAE regarded the family coup as a dangerous precedent to Gulf ruling families. Doha, running on gas, plotted its own role and deepened relations with Tehran. Qatar's version of austere Islam heightens its difference with Saudi Arabia by allowing women to drive and go about unveiled, and letting foreigners drink alcohol.[1]

A second piece published by the editorial board on 23 June, just two weeks after the outbreak of hostilities, doubled down on the publication's support for Al Jazeera, describing further calls to close down the network as "ridiculous" and categorizing them as part of a general assault on free speech in the Middle East. While acknowledging that some of Al Jazeera's past coverage must answer allegations of anti-Semitism and partisanship, the editorial made a point in stating that, overall, there is more free speech in Qatar than the UAE.[2]

In keeping with this tone, the *Guardian* also published two op-eds by Wadah Khanfar, the former director-general of Qatar's Al Jazeera network. Together, these pieces extolled the importance of Al Jazeera to the Middle Eastern media landscape and criticized the terrorist allegations made against Qatar as far-fetched, and primarily intended as a vehicle for Saudi Arabia to re-assert control in the region.[3]

An opinion piece published on 7 June, two days after the start of the crisis, by former Newsday Middle East Bureau Chief Mohamad Bazzi also focused primarily on questioning the competence of President Trump. Specifically, it argued that Saudi Arabia had successfully managed to exploit Trump by flattering his ego during his visit to the country in May 2017.

1 Editorial, 'The Guardian view on Trump's Middle East: unsafe,' *The Guardian*, 7 June 2017.

2 Editorial, 'The Guardian view on al-Jazeera: muzzling journalism,' *The Guardian*, 23 June 2017.

3 Wadah Khanfar, 'The blockade of Qatar is a move against the values of the Arab spring,' *The Guardian*, 8 June 2017; Wadah Khanfar, 'Al-Jazeera gave Arab youth a voice. Gulf regimes must not silence it,' *The Guardian*, 26 June 2017.

The author took a largely negative position on Saudi Arabia's manipulation of the US president (and the region) in a way that implied support for Qatar, and even accused Riyadh of trying to "force its smaller neighbor into submission." Bazzi also called Qatar an ally of the United States and, importantly, reminded readers that although Qatar has funded the Muslim Brotherhood and other extremist groups, "other Arab monarchies, including Saudi Arabia, also have a record of supporting extremists."[1]

The neutral pieces published by the *Guardian* took a more detached view of the crisis. Like in the *Telegraph*, some discussed the blockade only in terms of its impact on sports worldwide. Other op-eds detailed the grievances that exist on both sides of the conflict without, for the most part, delivering a strong judgment in favor of either party. Two pieces however, written separately by Paul Mason and Peter Salisbury, did clarify that Saudi Arabia has also been accused of financing terrorist organizations. These pieces also include some language that could be described as portraying Qatar in either a somewhat positive or negative light, depending on one's inclinations or interpretation of the text. For instance, both described Qatar as a country that "punches above its weight," a cliché used by many American and British news outlets when reporting on the tiny but influential country.[2] Furthermore, it should be noted that Paul Mason's piece, though refraining from expressing support for Qatar within the context of the crisis, did conclude with a decidedly negative view of British-Saudi relations.[3]

A comparison of the *Telegraph* and *Guardian* highlights the considerably different position taken by editorialists at the two news publications on the matter of Qatar's responsibility and blame for the blockade. A significant number of editorials at the conservative *Telegraph* did not hesitate to castigate Qatar for its role in the crisis, often criticizing or even blaming the country for allegedly financing Islamists and extremists, while for the most part ignoring Saudi Arabia's alleged similar dealings. Editorials at the liberal

---

1   Mohamad Bazzi, 'Saudi Arabia stroked Trump's ego. Now he is doing their bidding with Qatar,' *The Guardian*, 7 June 2017.

2   Paul Mason, 'The Qatar spat exposes Britain's game of thrones in the Gulf,' *The Guardian*, 5 June 2017; Peter Salisbury, 'It's Qatar v Saudi Arabia. But the west can't afford to pick a side,' *The Guardian*, 6 June 2017.

3   Paul Mason, 'The Qatar spat exposes Britain's game of thrones in the Gulf,' *The Guardian*, 5 June 2017.

Guardian, however, were more sympathetic to Qatar, still often criticizing the country but also calling out the misdeeds of the blockading countries. Columnists at the *Guardian* also seemed more willing to defend the value of Qatar's Al Jazeera news network and appeared supportive of Qatar's determination to protect its political sovereignty in the face of Saudi encroachment.

US Publications

One can see similar patterns emerging in the US publications examined in this study. A comparison of print opinion pieces on the Fox News website, known for its conservative editorial slant, and CNN, viewed as liberal in its punditry, shows that editorialists at the former have been highly suspicious of Qatar and generally more supportive of Saudi Arabia since the start of the blockade. Columnists at CNN, however, have taken a more balanced approach. Of the five opinion pieces published by Fox News that discussed the blockade in the relevant period, all criticized and none expressed sympathy or support for Qatar. In fact, three expressed overt support for Saudi Arabia.

An op-ed published on 13 June by Jim Hanson, the president of the Security Studies Group, took a negative view of Qatar, criticizing the country for its alleged terrorist financing while brushing off the significance of similar behavior by the Saudis:

> Qatar is far from the only one smiling at us while doling out satchels of cash to the bad guys. The Saudis are arguably worse, but you have to start somewhere and President Trump determined he could enlist the Saudis in this endeavor. This is a version of that French Foreign Legion tactic pour encourager les autres, where one malefactor is chosen for a very public punishment "to encourage the others" toward better behavior.[1]

Likewise, Ali Shihabi of the Arabia Foundation think tank in Washington, D.C., completely glossed over any sort of Saudi culpability for the crisis. In an opinion piece published on 21 June, he praised the new Saudi crown

---

1   Jim Hanson, 'Qatar must choose a side in the global fight against Islamic terror,' Fox News Opinion, 13 June 2017.

prince and heir to the throne, Mohammed bin Salman, for his pro-Ameri-canism, his reforming efforts at home, and for having improved US-Saudi relations in the first year of the Trump presidency. He also argued that Saudi Arabia's central role in the coalition against Qatar, which he described as having "long openly backed anti-American Islamist groups," is possibly the result of the prince's desire "to support the president's call" for American allies in the region to take the lead in suppressing extremism. He made no mention of any past or present Saudi connections to extremist groups or terror financing.[1]

Jim Hanson painted a similar picture in a 5 December opinion piece. The headline advertises his view upfront: "Change in the Middle East must come from people in the region – that's why I support new Saudi moves." In this piece, he described Saudi Arabia as Washington's long-time ally and also extolled the progressive credentials of the new heir apparent both inside and outside the kingdom. He praised the blockade as having "struck a blow against Qatari terror financing and that is a good thing. The diplomatic disruption has our State Department in a tizzy trying to find any way to resolve this, but thus far President Trump has been satisfied to let it play out."[2]

One particularly forceful opinion piece was written on 1 December by Charles Wald, a former US Air Force general. Wald asserted that the US could do without an air force base in Qatar and could easily find another convenient location, and he supported the decision to do so "if Qatar won't support our fight against terrorism." He then described Qatar's foreign policy as "schizophrenic" and noted that it "has a long history of providing sanctuary to terrorist leaders, including Sept. 11 mastermind Khalid Sheikh Mohammed." He went on to criticize Al Jazeera, including its coverage of the Bahrain uprisings in 2011, which he implied were Iranian-backed "protests," before concluding:

> Qatar has a choice to make. It can choose to be a U.S. ally that
> confronts all terrorists and extremists and joins the U.S. in actually

1   Ali Shihabi, 'Saudi Crown Prince Mohammed bin Salman's appointment is chance to re-set US relations following nadir of the Obama administration,' Fox News Opinion, 21 June 2017.

2   Jim Hanson, 'Change in the Middle East change must come from people in the region – that's why I support new Saudi moves,' Fox News Opinion, 5 December 2017.

aligning on national security issues against Iran and its proxies – or it can continue a two-faced foreign policy.

Whatever path Qatar chooses, American policymakers need to remember that the U.S. has never been and never will be dependent on a military presence at Al-Udeid Air Base. We need to put Qatar's rulers on notice that if they don't shape up, we can easily ship out. [1]

On the other hand, print editorials on the CNN website over the same time period did not speak so emotively on the issue of the blockade. Of some 28 published pieces that mentioned the diplomatic crisis in some way, only eight took particularly strong views either for or against Qatar; six expressed sympathy or positive attitudes toward Qatar and two were largely negative.

The 20 remaining op-eds can best be described as neutral when it comes to favoring either side of the conflict, with many referencing the blockade as part of a wider discussion regarding President Trump and/or international politics. For instance, an opinion piece published on 8 June by Simon Mabon, a lecturer in the International Relations of the Middle East at Lancaster University, offered a detached, academic perspective on the burgeoning crisis. Though presented as an editorial, it is more of a balanced piece of analysis that attempts to clarify the context of the crisis, the events and foreign policy choices that led to it, and the viewpoints of the main players – Saudi Arabia and Qatar.

Mabon used dispassionate terms to describe the various issues at stake. For example, he noted that Doha's support for the Muslim Brotherhood "has been viewed with a great deal of suspicion across the region." Similar to the *Guardian* View editorial mentioned above, he also clarified the motives behind Qatar's alleged cooperation with the Taliban, writing that the "Qataris have also attempted to facilitate dialogue between the Taliban and the US." He concluded with a rather detached observation that "It appears that almost 40 years after the formation of the GCC, Saudi Arabia is increasingly of the opinion that its friend is deceiving them and that Qatar must be treated like an enemy."[2]

---

1   Charles Wald, 'US doesn't need Qatar air base if Qatar won't support our fight against terrorism,' Fox News Opinion, 1 December 2017.

2   Simon Mabon, 'Iran, Saudi Arabia and the Gulf: A tangled web of politics and terror,' CNN, 8 June 2017.

A 27 July editorial piece by Frida Ghitis, a world affairs columnist, can be classified as somewhat negative toward Qatar. It called for the Trump administration to speak with a clear and united voice when dealing with the crisis. She described Qatar as having "played a dual role – helping fight terrorism on one hand, while backing groups with extremist ideology on the other." And like the two *Guardian* columnists, she explained how the country has used its wealth to "punch above its weight on the global scene." One of her most passionate statements laid down a challenge to Qatar, in arguing that it "will have to decide where it stands."[1] Yet, though critical of Qatar, even so the piece lacked the strong rhetoric featured in the Fox News editorials examined above.

Two op-eds published just days apart, however, did present strong view points for or against Qatar. On 20 June, the UAE's Minister of State, Sultan Ahmed Al Jaber, wrote that Qatar must "change its behavior" and adhere to the 2014 Riyadh agreement it signed along with other GCC partners to promote cooperation on counter-terrorism. He continued,

> People should know that our decision to cut ties was taken with a heavy heart. It has consequences that its neighbors must bear alongside the State of Qatar. Our people have friends and relatives in Qatar, who have been affected by this. However, we all risk a much greater peril were we not to act …We want nothing more than to resume normal, respectful and friendly relations with Qatar. A diplomatic solution is attainable, but the key to that outcome lies with the government of Qatar. Doha's decision makers have a choice to make. They can lead their country to the fold of civilized nations, or continue down a destructive and isolating path. I truly hope they change course and choose wisely.[2]

On the other hand, on 23 June, Chris Doyle, the director of the policy and advocacy group the Council for Arab-British Understanding (CAABU), demonstrated clear support for Qatar. The demands of the blockading countries, he argued, are "absurdly over the top" and are a ruse intended to

---

1   Frida Ghitis, 'Middle East madness engulfs Iran, Qatar and US,' CNN, 7 June 2017.

2   Sultan Ahmed Al Jaber, 'Qatar must stop changing the subject -- and start changing its behavior,' CNN, 20 June 2017.

re-instate "Saudi dominance in the region." In addition, he also challenged the claims of the boycotting countries:

> A litany of allegations against Qatar have flooded the media, the vast majority of which, as yet, are not backed up by any credible evidence. These have been followed by a set of demands that are virtually impossible for Qatar to meet. Some of the allegations demonstrate rank hypocrisy. Saudi accusations against Qatar risk shining a light on to the Saudis' own historic funding of extremist groups and intolerant ideologies.[1]

Conclusion and Lessons Learned

This chapter is intended to provide an initial analysis and understanding of how some commentators and columnists at conservative and liberal media outlets in the United States and United Kingdom have covered the blockade over its first nine months. It is not intended to paint a comprehensive picture of the coverage of the crisis at these news sites or across the wider media.

However, based on the above analysis, it appears that conservative media pundits and editorials, specifically those published in the *Telegraph* and Fox News, have expressed stronger and more robustly negative attitudes toward Qatar and stronger support for Saudi Arabia on the matter of the legitimacy and necessity of the blockade. These same pundits have also appeared more willing to play down or gloss over allegations of Saudi support and financing of Islamist extremists, but have not hesitated to call out Qatar for similar behavior.

The more liberal media, specifically the *Guardian* and CNN, seems to take a more sympathetic and/or balanced approach, detailing bad behavior on all sides of the conflict and, on several occasions, providing what appears to be a more detached, comprehensive analysis of the situation. That said, these conservative and liberal outlets have also provided a platform for opposing viewpoints. Notably, the *Telegraph* published an opinion piece by Qatar's ambassador in London and CNN published one by an Emirati minister.

---

1   Chris Doyle, 'Qatar crisis is a mess the Middle East could do without,' CNN, 23 June 2017.

Index

Africa, 141–51
   GCC investments, 143
   securitization, 145, 148
Al Jazeera, 57, 87, 101, 147, 153, 182
Al-Ittihad, 166–78
Al-Thani, Sheikh Hamad bin Khalifa, 17, 21, 89, 100
Al-Thani, Sheikh Mohammed bin Abdulrahman, 160, 162, 177
Al-Thani, Sheikh Tamim bin Hamad, 21, 67, 115, 154
Al-Thani, Sheikha Al Mayassa bint Hamad, 14, 19, 22
Bedaya, 43
Bloomberg, 173, 174
Carnegie Mellon University in Qatar, 44
citizenship, laws, 61, 66, 67
climate change, 135, 136, 138, 139
CNN, 185, 187, 190
cyber security, 107–19
   attacks on Qatar, 108, 113
   education and research, 117
   fundamentals, 107
   internet backbone, 110
   Kahramaa, 118
Djibouti, 148
Doha International Center for Interfaith Dialogue, 55
electricity market, GCC, 134
energy cooperation, 131, 132
energy poverty, 130, 131
energy security, 131, 132, 138

energy, water and food (EWF) nexus, 26, 35, 36

entrepreneurship, 37–48

   country rankings, 38

   ecosystems, 41

   non-economic variables, 47

   societal responses, 44

food imports, 27

   meat and dairy, 34

food security, 24–36

food self-sufficiency, 31, 33, 34, 35

food systems

   availability, 27

   description, 24

   geography, 25

   resilience, 29, 35

Foreign Policy Analysis, 94–106

   role conceptions, 96, 99

Forum for Promoting Peace in Muslim Societies, 54

Fox News, 185, 190

Gas Exporting Countries Forum, 133

GCC Interconnection Authority (GCCIA), 131, 134

grand mufti, Egypt, 52, 57

grand mufti, Saudi Arabia, 52, 54

Guardian, 179, 182, 183, 184, 190

Hamad Bin Khalifa University, 45, 73, 77, 78

Hamad Port, 32

Hassad Food, 31, 32

HBKU Souqna, 45

INJAZ Qatar, 43

International Union of Muslim Scholars, 56

Iran, 90, 91, 145, 146

labor reforms, 62, 68

maṣlaḥa, 52

Mathaf, 17, 20

media coverage, UK and US, 179–90

Mohammed bin Salman (MBS), 102, 144, 146

Mohammed bin Zayed (MBZ), 102, 146

Museum of Islamic Art, 17

Muslim Brotherhood, 56, 57, 90, 101, 103, 147, 177

Nama, 43

National Interest online magazine, 171

National Museum of Qatar, 21, 22

natural gas, 120–29
    Dolphin pipeline, 121, 123, 134
    GCC, 121, 127
    international markets, 122, 124, 139
    North Field, 126
    oversupply, 125

Organization of the Petroleum Exporting Countries (OPEC), 120, 132

Qaradawi, Sheikh Yusuf, 56, 58

Qatar Business Incubation Center, 43

Qatar Chamber, 43

Qatar Development Bank, 42

Qatar Finance and Business Academy, 43

Qatar Foundation, 72–81
    history, 72
    vision, 72, 79

Qatar Museums, 16, 17, 21
    Mal Lawal, 18

Qatar National Research Fund, 39

Qatar National Vision 2030, 37, 42, 47, 136

Qatar News Agency, 113, 114, 154

Qatar University, 44

Ramadan, 49, 154

religion in foreign policy, 49–59

Shura Council, 68, 69

Silatech, 43

small state behavior, 83–93
  larger powers, 85, 86, 88, 97
Somalia, 149, 150
Sudan, 147
Telegraph, 179, 180, 181, 190
Torba Farmers Market, 45
Turkey, 90
Twitter, 153–65
United States, 88
  Donald Trump, 103, 153
value-added tax, 63
virtual water, 28